The Fountain of Paradise

Fāṭima al-Zahrā' in the Quran

The Tafsīr of Sūrah al-Insān, Sūrah al-Qadr, and Sūrah al-Kawthar

Compiled by a Group of Muslim Scholars under the guidance of Ayatullah Nasir Makarim Shirazi

Translated by Saleem Bhimji

Edited by Arifa Hudda

ISBN: 978-1-927930-51-9

The Fountain of Paradise: Fāṭima al-Zahrā' ﷺ in the Noble Quran
The Tafsīr of Sūrah al-Insān, Sūrah al-Qadr, and Sūrah al-Kawthar

Compiled by a Group of Muslim Scholars under the guidance of
Ayatullah Nasir Makarim Shirazi

Translated by Saleem Bhimji
Edited by Arifa Hudda

Published by Islamic Publishing House
www.iph.ca · iph@iph.ca

Cover Design and Layout by Saleem Bhimji for the Islamic Publishing House

Transliteration Table

The method of transliteration of Islamic terminology from the ʿArabic language has been carried out according to the standard transliteration table mentioned below.

ء	ʾ	س	s	م	m
ا	a	ش	sh	ن	n
ب	b	ص	ṣ	و	w
ت	t	ض	ḍ	ه	h
ث	th	ط	ṭ	ي	y
ج	j	ظ	ḍ		
ح	ḥ	ع	ʿ		
خ	kh	غ	gh		
د	d	ف	f		
ذ	dh	ق	q		
ر	r	ك	k		
ز	z	ل	l		

Short Vowels

ـَـ	a
ـِـ	i
ـُـ	u

Long Vowels

ا	ā
ي	ī
و	ū

Dedication

This work is dedicated to a lady who holds the distinction of being the 'Leader of the Women of All of the Worlds' - from the first to the last - Lady Fāṭima al-Zahrā' ﷺ.

Fāṭima al-Zahrā' ﷺ has the honour of being the only surviving child of the final Messenger of Allah, Prophet Muḥammad ﷺ, and as such, her status is even further elevated - as it is through her that the lineage of the Prophet continues until the end of time.

May Allah ﷻ accept this humble effort from all of those involved in this project, and may He make this book the means through which Fāṭima al-Zahrā' ﷺ finds us worthy of her intercession on the Day of Judgement.

Table of Contents

Introduction by the Translator i

Sūrah al-Insān (Sūrah al-Dahr) 11

Contents of Sūrah al-Insān 11
Place of Revelation 11
Merits of Recitation of Sūrah al-Insān 14

Section One - Verses 1 to 4 17

Transformation and Guidance 17
Tumultuous World of the Fetus 24

Section Two - Verses 5 to 11 27

Status of the Ahlul Bayt ﷺ 27
Great Reward for the Righteous 34
Feeding the Hungry 45

Section Three - Verses 12 to 22 49

Great Rewards of Paradise 50

Section Four - Verses 23 to 26 65

Five Points for Success 65

Section Five - Verses 27 to 31 71

This is a Warning Call 71

Sūrah al-Qadr 81

Contents of Sūrah al-Qadr 81
Virtues of Studying this Chapter 81

Section One - Verses 1 to 5 83

Revelation of the Quran 83
What is Determined on that Night? 91
When is the Night of Qadr? 93
Why Keep the Date Hidden? 95
Night of Qadr in Previous Communities 96
Better than One Thousand Months? 97

Why Reveal the Quran on That Night? 97
Is the Night of Qadr the Same Night Globally? 98
Fāṭima al-Zahrā' **is** the Night of Qadr 99
How is Fāṭima al-Zahrā' ﷺ al-Qadr? 100

Sūrah al-Kawthar 107

Contents of Sūrah al-Kawthar 107
Virtue of Studying this Chapter 109

Section One - Verses 1 to 3 111

We have Given You Much Goodness 111
What is al-Kawthar? 112
Fāṭima al-Zahrā' ﷺ and al-Kawthar 116
The Miracle of this Chapter 118
Allah ﷻ and the Plural Pronoun 119

Various Ziyārāt for Fāṭima al-Zahrā' ﷺ 121

Ziyārah One 121
Ziyārah Two 128
Ziyārah for the 3rd of Jumādī al-Ākhir 137
Ziyārah on Sunday 138

Other Publications Available 139

بسم الله الرحمن الرحيم

In the Name of Allah, the All-Compassionate, the All-Merciful

Introduction by the Translator

What follows in this book is a commentary of three specific chapters from the Noble Quran which speak about the spiritual greatness and significance of the only daughter of Prophet Muḥammad ﷺ, Fāṭima al-Zahrā' ؑ.

Translated from the original Farsi work which was compiled by a Group of Muslim Scholars under the guidance of Āyatullāh Nāṣir Makārim Shīrāzī, and other sources to complete the discussion in certain areas as have been indicated, this publication adds merely a drop into the endless ocean of the pre-eminence of the Ahlul Bayt ؑ in the Noble Quran, and specifically the direct and indirect mention of the Leader of the Women of all the Worlds, Fāṭima al-Zahrā' ؑ, as spoken by Allah ﷻ.

Every year, millions of Muslims around the world remember Fāṭima al-Zahrā' ؑ on a regular basis. There are a multitude of gatherings - both commemorations and mourning ceremonies in her memory. There are observances of praise, joy, and honour for her in which her noble characteristics are remembered; and Muslims also hold rituals of lamentation where they recount - in vivid detail - the painful events of Islamic history which led to her intense grief and eventual martyrdom. The faithful even go to the extent of invoking Allah ﷻ to deprive those who hurt her from His Mercy and Blessings!

Despite everything which is recalled on the pulpits throughout the world, and the articles and booklets which have been published so far about this great woman, the true history of her short life and the salient features of her personality are still unknown; however, with the little that the Muslims know about her, we still accept the fact that Fāṭima al-Zahrā' ﷺ holds a very lofty spiritual status.

The sphere of influence of this great lady ﷺ is extensive, and she not only appeals and is a person of reverence for the entire Muslim community, nor is she such that only Muslim authors have written about her - rather, her character, personality, and visage transcend religion and the Muslim sphere.

In her work, *Chosen among Women: Mary and Fatima in Medieval Christianity and Shi'ite Islam*, Mary Thurlkill writes the following about the beloved daughter of Prophet Muḥammad ﷺ:

> According to early medieval Christian and Shi'ite tradition, God chose Mary and Fatima as vessels for His sublime progeny. Mary, an obedient maiden gave birth to the God-Man Jesus; Fatima, sharing in the divine *nur*, held the Imamate within her womb...
>
> Theologians clearly relied on Mary and Fatima to articulate and expand their respective orthodoxies and notions of rightness. By defining first their pure and immaculate nature, authors transformed Mary's and Fatima's bodies into sacred containers...
>
> Fatima also served as a sacred vessel, holding the Imam's *nur* within her, while simultaneously sharing it. Fatima al-Zahra existed as the only female member of the holy family, and like her father, husband, and sons, remained immaculate and infallible. Both Shi'ite and Christian authors also likened their holy women to an ancient container, Noah's ark; the women's wombs carried humanity's true salvation. Mary and Fatima served equally crucial functions in political and sectarian discourse. With such a rhetorical agenda in mind, hagiographers accented Mary's and Fatima's maternal roles. These holy women, as mothers, effectively defined the limits of community and sectarian division.

> By symbolically adopting believers to their maternal care, Mary and Fatima damned unbelievers to hell. Hagiographers advertised their holy mothers by describing their homey miracles and domestic skills. Both women experienced superhuman parturitions, multiplied food, and interceded for their spiritual offspring...
>
> Fatima, the mystical nexus of the holy family, rewards her adoptive kin who weep for her slain son, Husayn, and escorts women into paradise on judgement day. Because these women (Mary and Fatima) are both powerful, yet intimately connected to domestic (private) space, they can be employed by authors for a variety of purposes.
>
> Mary and Fatima can signify both female independence and agency and submission and chastity ... whether in the seventh century or the twenty-first, Mary's and Fatima's charisma affords scholars and religious alike an important symbol of community and religiosity that may be manipulated in several ways.
>
> The holy women's attendance within the home subtly stresses the male households' presence and dominance. In the end, however, Mary and Fatima - chosen by God as holy vessels and chosen by men as didactic models - manage to provide moral exemplars for women, promote standards of sanctity and faith, and chastise religious and political heresy. Within such legacies the domestic indeed complements public (masculine) authority and gains a place for feminine sanctity not easily ignored.[1]

The Prophet of Islam ﷺ who speaks nothing but what has been revealed to him or is ordered to say by Allah Himself ﷻ, mentioned

---

[1] *Chosen among Women: Mary and Fatima in Medieval Christianity and Shi'ite Islam*; written by Mary F. Thurlkill; Printed by University of Notre Dame Press 2007; Pp. 119-123.

the following glowing tributes regarding his beloved daughter, Fāṭima al-Zahrā' 🌺:

- "On the Day of Judgement, a caller will call out: 'Lower your gaze until Fāṭima has passed.'"[2]
- "I am not pleased unless Fāṭima is pleased."[3]
- "The most beloved of my family to me is Fāṭima."[4]
- "The head of the women of Paradise is Fāṭima."[5]
- "Many men have reached completion, but no women have reached completion except for four: Maryam, Āsiya, Khadījah, and Fāṭima."[6]
- "The Verse of Purification (Quran, Sūrah al-Aḥzāb (33), verse 33) was revealed concerning five people: myself, ʿAlī, Ḥasan, Ḥusayn, and Fāṭima."[7]
- "Fāṭima is part of me. Whatever upsets her, upsets me, and whatever harms her, harms me."[8]

---

[2] *Kanz al-ʿUmmāl*, Vol. 13, Pp. 91 & 93, *Muntakhab Kanz al-ʿUmmāl* quoted in the margin of *Al-Musnad*, Vol. 5, Pg. 96; *Al-Sawāʾiq al-Muhariqa*, Pg. 190; *ʿUsd al-Ghāba*, Vol. 5, Pg. 523; *Tadhkirat al-Khawwāṣ*, Pg. 279; *Dhakāʾir al-ʿUqbā*, Pg. 48; *Manāqib al-Imām ʿAlī* of Ibn al-Maghāzalī, Pg. 356; *Nūr al-Abṣār*, Pp. 51-52, *Yanābīʿ al-Mawadda*, Vol. 2, Chap. 56, Pg. 136.

[3] *Manāqib al-Imām ʿAlī* of Ibn al-Maghāzalī, Pg. 342.

[4] *Al-Jāmīʿ al-Ṣaghīr*, Vol. 1, Trad. #203, Pg. 37; *Al-Sawāʾiq al-Muhariqa*, Pg. 191; *Yanābīʿ al-Mawadda*, Vol. 2, Chap. 59, Pg. 479; *Kanz al-ʿUmmāl*, Vol. 13, Pg. 93.

[5] *Kanz al-ʿUmmāl*, Vol. 13, Pg. 94; *Ṣaḥīḥ al-Bukhārī*, *Kitāb al-Fadhāʾil*, Chapter on the Virtues of Fāṭima; *Al-Bidāya wa al-Nihāya*, Vol. 2, Pg. 61.

[6] *Nūr al-Abṣār*, Pg. 51.

[7] *Isʿaf al-Rāghibīn*, Pg. 116; *Ṣaḥīḥ al-Muslim*, *Kitāb Fadhāʾil al-Ṣaḥāba*.

[8] *Ṣaḥīḥ al-Muslim*, Vol. 5, Pg. 54; *Khaṣāʾis al-Imām ʿAlī* of al-Nisāʾī, Pp. 121-122; *Maṣābīḥ al-Sunnah*, Vol. 4, Pg. 185; *Al-Iṣābah*, Vol. 4, Pg. 378; *Seir ʿAlam al-Nubalāʾ*, Vol. 2, Pg. 119; *Kanz al-ʿUmmāl*, Vol. 13, Pg. 97; Similar wording is related in *Al-Tirmidhī*, Vol. 3, Chapter on the Virtues of Fāṭima, Pg. 241; *Ḥaliyat al-Awliyāʾ*, Vol. 2, Pg. 40; *Muntakhab Kanz al-*

- "Fāṭima is part of me, and whoever pleases her, pleases me."[9]
- "O Fāṭima, verily Allah is angry when you are angry."[10]

These and hundreds of other Prophetic statements and numerous verses of the Noble Quran give us a glimpse into this great woman and oblige us to study her life and the legacy she left behind.

It is indeed exceedingly difficult to speak about the personality of Lady Fāṭima al-Zahrā' ﷺ - she is the role model that Islam wants all women to follow. She is a symbol of the various dimensions of womanhood. She is the perfect model of a daughter when dealing with her parents; the perfect model of a wife when dealing with her husband; the perfect model of a mother when raising her children; and the perfect model of an enthusiastic, strong, fighting woman when confronting her adversaries and the oppressions in her society. Fāṭima al-Zahrā' ﷺ herself is a guide - an outstanding example of someone to follow, an ideal type of woman - one whose life bore witness for any woman who wishes to 'become herself' and regain her own identity.

Her life was wrought with many difficulties: losing her mother when she was only five years old; being brought up by her father (the Messenger of Allah ﷺ) who had the added responsibility of being the final Prophet of Allah ﷻ; the physical aggression and mental torture which the polytheists wreaked on her family, friends, and the believers; and ultimately, having to leave her city

---

'Ummāl, in the margins of *Al-Musnad*, Vol. 5, Pg. 96; *Ma'rifat mā Yajib li 'ala Āl-Bayt al-Nabawī min al-Ḥaqq 'alā man A'dāhum*, Pg. 58; *Dhakā'ir al-'Uqbā*, Pg. 38; *Tadhkirat al-Khawāṣ*, Pg. 279; *Yanābī' al-Mawadda*, Vol. 2, Chap. 59, Pg. 478.

[9] *Al-Sawā'iq al-Muhariqa*, Pp. 132 & 180; *Mustadrak al-Ḥākim*; *Ma'rifat mā Yajib li 'ala Āl Bayt al-Nabawi min al-Ḥaqq 'alā man A'dāhum*, Pg. 73; *Yanābī' al-Mawadda*, Vol. 2, Chap. 59, Pg. 468.

[10] *Al-Sawā'iq al-Muhariqa*, Pg. 175; *Mustadrak al-Ḥākim*, Chapter on the Virtues of Fāṭima; *Manāqib al-Imām 'Alī* of Ibn al-Maghāzalī, Pg. 351.

of birth of Mecca and migrate to a new home and community hundreds of kilometers to the north in the city of Medina.

Eventually, she had to witness the death (or according to most reports, the poisoning and murder) of her father, and the masses vying for political authority - leaving his lifeless body to take part in elections; followed by the rejection of her husband, Imām ʿAlī and his Prophetically and Divinely-granted authority over the community by the majority of Muslims; and tragically in the end, the physical attacks against her which resulted in her miscarrying the son (Muḥsin) in her womb, several broken ribs, and her untimely martyrdom at the tender age of only eighteen years.

Fāṭima al-Zahrāʾ lived like this and died like this - however, even after her death, she began a new chapter in history.

The memory of Fāṭima al-Zahrāʾ grows through the love of the people who throughout history, have fought for freedom and justice. All over the centuries, innocent people have been punished under the merciless and bloody lash of various governments. Their cries and anger grew and overflowed from their wounded hearts, and that is why in the history of all spiritually awakened and knowledgeable Islamic communities, Fāṭima al-Zahrāʾ has been the source of inspiration for those who want to reclaim their rights, for those who seek justice, and for those who resist oppression, cruelty, and discrimination.

She was not just a wife to Imām ʿAlī, rather he looked upon her as a best friend - a friend who was familiar with his pains and aspirations. She was his endless refuge, the one who listened to his secrets, and the one who was his true companion in his loneliness. This is why Imām ʿAlī behaved slightly differently towards her and her children compared to the other wives that he married after his beloved's death, and the other children whom he fathered. After Lady Fāṭima died, Imām ʿAlī married other women and had children from them; but from the very beginning, he separated the children who were from Fāṭima from his other children - the latter were called 'Banū ʿAlī' (lit. the children of ʿAlī), while the former were referred to as 'Banū Fāṭima' (lit. the children of Fāṭima).

In closing, we would first like to thank Allah ﷻ for bestowing upon us the Divine providence *(tawfīq)* to be able to complete the publication of this work, as without His constant guidance and blessings, we would not be where we are today. We also pray for the intercession of Prophet Muḥammad ﷺ and his noble family members, the Ahlul Bayt (عليهم السلام); and implore the Highest to continue to bless them and raise their ranks in Paradise, and that they accept this noble publication as our humble attempt to keep alive their memory and teachings.

We would also like to acknowledge the support, encouragement, and assistance of Sr. Arifa Hudda, specifically for her review and editing of this book.

Finally, we would like to appreciate and thank the donor who generously donated to publish the initial edition of this book.

May Allah ﷻ bless everyone and accept the intercession of Lady Fāṭima al-Zahrā' (عليها السلام) for all of us for whatever little services we do in her memory.

Saleem Bhimji
December 17th, 2023 CE
Jumādī al-Ākhir 3rd, 1445 AH
Martyrdom Anniversary of Fāṭima al-Zahrā' (عليها السلام)

Fāṭima al-Zahrāʾ عليها السلام in the Noble Quran

Sūrah al-Insān (also known as Sūrah al-Dahr)

The Chapter of Humanity or *The Time*

This chapter was revealed in Medina and contains 31 verses

Sūrah al-Insān (Sūrah al-Dahr)

Contents of Sūrah al-Insān

Although this chapter is short, its contents are deep, multi-faceted and comprehensive, and can be divided into five sections:

1. The creation of the human being, and their origin as a drop of sperm (along with the egg); followed by the guidance which one has been given, and the freedom of choice to do as one pleases.
2. The reward given to the righteous doers - the history of revelation of this section is related to the Ahlul Bayt ﷺ - which we will discuss in depth.
3. The reasons why these righteous doers (the Ahlul Bayt ﷺ) deserve the reward that they were given, which is explained using short, yet powerful verses.
4. The importance of the Quran and how to implement its legislations, along with the various difficulties on the path of self-reformation.
5. The overall rule of the Will of Allah ﷻ (while at the same time attesting to the freedom of choice that human beings have).

Various names have been mentioned for this chapter, the most famous of them being: *'Al-Insān'* - 'Humanity;' *'Al-Dahr'* - 'The Time;' and *'Hal Atā'* - 'Has there come;' and each of these have been extracted from the words contained in the first few verses of this chapter. However, as we will soon see regarding the merits of recitation of this chapter, in the traditions, it has only been referred to as *'Hal Atā.'*

Place of Revelation

The place of revelation for this chapter - whether it was in Medina or Mecca - is a discussion among the exegetes of the Quran.

The consensus of the scholars and exegetes from the Shīʿa tradition is that this entire chapter, or at least the beginning section in which the status of these righteous individuals (the Ahlul Bayt ﷺ) and the actions of these noble personalities have been mentioned was revealed in Medina. These verses form the basis of a historical event regarding an oath made by Imām ʿAlī ﷺ, his wife Lady Fāṭima al-Zahrā' ﷺ, their children - Imām Ḥasan ﷺ and Imām Ḥusayn ﷺ, and their housekeeper Fiḍḍah, which we will mention in more detail a bit later.

In addition, it well-known among the scholars of the Ahl al-Sunnah that the revelation of these verses was in Medina, just as al-Qurṭubī mentioned: *The well-known opinion of the scholars is that it was revealed in Medina.*[11]

The following scholars consider some or even a part of this chapter as being revealed in Medina:

1. Ḥākim Abūl Qāsim al-Ḥaskānī narrates from Ibn ʿAbbās in regard to the number of verses which were revealed in Mecca and Medina, and states that this chapter was revealed in Medina after Sūrah al-Raḥmān (55), before Sūrah al-Ṭalāq (65).[12]

The author of *Al-Ayḍhāḥ*, Aḥmad al-Zāhid, also narrates this same opinion from Ibn ʿAbbās.[13]

2. In the book, *History of the Quran,* written by Abū ʿAbdillāh al-Zanjānī, who took his information from *Nazm Durr wa Tanāsurul Ayāt wa Suwar*, it is mentioned that a group of prominent scholars of the Ahl al-Sunnah have narrated that Sūrah al-Insān is among those chapters which were revealed in Medina.[14]

---

[11] *Tafsīr al-Qurṭubī*, Vol. 10, Pg. 6909.

[12] *Tafsīr Majmaʿ al-Bayān*, Vol. 10, Pg. 405.

[13] Ibid.

[14] *Tārikh al-Quran*, Pg. 55.

3. In the book, *Al-Fihrist*, of Ibn Nadīm, it has been narrated from Ibn ʿAbbās that Sūrah *Hal Atā* was the eleventh chapter to be revealed in Medina.[15]

4. In *Al-Itqān* of al-Suyūṭī, it has been mentioned from al-Bayhaqī, as seen in *Dalāʾil al-Nubuwwah* from ʿAkramah that the chapter *Hal Atā* was revealed in Medina.[16]

5. In the book, *Durr al-Manthūr*, the same tradition as mentioned above has been narrated from Ibn ʿAbbās from a different chain of narrators.[17]

6. Al-Zamakhsharī, in his work, *Tafsīr al-Kashshāf*, has narrated the well-known historical event for which the initial verses of this chapter were revealed as being regarding the vow taken by (Imām) ʿAlī ◈, his wife, and their children.[18]

7. In addition to the references stated above, many other prominent scholars of the Ahl al-Sunnah have also stated that the initial verses of this chapter were revealed in regard to (Imām) ʿAlī ◈, Fāṭima al-Zahrāʾ ◈, Ḥasan ◈, and Ḥusayn ◈, and this proves that this chapter was revealed in Medina, because both Imāms Ḥasan ◈ and Ḥusayn ◈ were born in Medina!

Other scholars who have stated this belief include: al-Wāḥidī in his work, *Asbāb al-Nuzūl*; al-Baghawī in his book, *Maʿālim al-Tanzīl*; Sibṭ ibn al-Jawzī in his work, *Al-Tadhkirah*; Ganjī al-Shāfiʿī in his work, *Kifāyat al-Ṭālib*, and others.[19]

This opinion is so well-known and acknowledged by the scholars that Muḥammad ibn Idrīs al-Shāfiʿī, one of the four Imāms of the Ahl al-Sunnah, composed the following poem:

---

[15] *Tārikh al-Quran*, Pg. 55.
[16] *Al-Mizān fī Tafsīr al-Quran*, Vol. 20, Pg. 221.
[17] Ibid.
[18] *Tafsīr al-Kashshāf*, Vol. 4, Pg. 670.
[19] *Aḥqāq al-Ḥaqq*, Vol. 3, Pp. 157 to 170, which has narrated the names of the scholars and the works in which they have written this information.

الى م الى م و حتى متى ؟   أعاتب فى حب هذا الفتى!

و هل زوجت فاطم غيره ؟   و فى غيره هل اتى هل اتى !؟

Till when, till when, and until what time?
Shall you rebuke me for loving this chivalrous man ('Alī)?
Did Fāṭima marry any other than him?
And was 'Hal Atā' revealed for other than him ('Alī)?[20]

There are numerous other references in these regards which we will mention under the discussion of the verses in this chapter.

However, with all of these proofs, there are still individuals who insist that this chapter was revealed in Mecca, and deny all of the traditions which speak about this chapter being revealed in Medina, and that this chapter was sent down in regards to 'Alī, Fāṭima, and their two children, Ḥasan and Ḥusayn!

It is astounding to see that anytime a verse or Prophetic tradition ends up proclaiming the virtues of Imām 'Alī and the Ahlul Bayt, a group of people stand up and raise a clamour and become very sensitive - as if Islam has fallen into danger if they were to accept these traditions! Seeing as how they claim that Imām 'Alī is among the 'Rightly Guided Caliphs' and is one of the great leaders of Islam, and that they have love for the Ahlul Bayt, then in our opinion, the animosity which they have stems from the days of rulership of the *Umayyad* empire and the negative propaganda of that era which has taken them over.

May Allah protect us all from such errors in our life!

Merits of Recitation of Sūrah al-Insān

It has been narrated from the Noble Prophet that:

---

[20] *Aḥqāq al-Ḥaqq*, Vol. 3, Pg. 158.

مَنْ قَرَأَ سُوْرَةُ ﴿هَلْ أَتَى﴾ كَانَ جَزَاؤُهُ عَلَى اللهِ جَنَّةً وَحَرِيرًا.

> "A person who recites the chapter of "*Hal Atā*," their reward with Allah will be Paradise and garments of silk."[21]

In a tradition from Imām Muḥammad al-Bāqir ﷺ, it has been stated that: "One of the rewards which will be granted to a person who recites the chapter of '*Hal Atā*' every Thursday morning is that on the Day of Resurrection, they will be alongside the Prophet."[22]

---

[21] *Tafsīr Majma*ʿ *al-Bayān*, Vol. 10, Pg. 402.

[22] Ibid.

بِسْمِ ٱللَّهِ ٱلرَّحْمَٰنِ ٱلرَّحِيمِ

In the Name of Allah, the All-Compassionate, the All-Merciful

Section One - Verses 1 to 4

﴿هَلْ أَتَىٰ عَلَى ٱلْإِنسَٰنِ حِينٌ مِّنَ ٱلدَّهْرِ لَمْ يَكُن شَيْـًٔا مَّذْكُورًا ﴿١﴾ إِنَّا خَلَقْنَا
ٱلْإِنسَٰنَ مِن نُّطْفَةٍ أَمْشَاجٍ نَّبْتَلِيهِ فَجَعَلْنَٰهُ سَمِيعًۢا بَصِيرًا ﴿٢﴾ إِنَّا هَدَيْنَٰهُ
ٱلسَّبِيلَ إِمَّا شَاكِرًا وَإِمَّا كَفُورًا ﴿٣﴾ إِنَّآ أَعْتَدْنَا لِلْكَٰفِرِينَ سَلَٰسِلَا۟ وَأَغْلَٰلًا
وَسَعِيرًا ﴿٤﴾﴾

"Has there not come over the human being a period when they were a thing not worth mentioning? Surely, We have created the human being from a small life-germ uniting (itself): We mean to try them, so We have made them hearing (and) seeing. Surely, We have shown them the way: they may be thankful or unthankful. Surely, We have prepared for the unbelievers: chains and shackles and a burning fire."

Transformation and Guidance

Although most of the discussions in this chapter of the Quran revolve around the Day of Resurrection and the blessings contained in Paradise, the beginning of this sūrah focuses on the creation of a human being because if we pay close attention to the creation of the human being, then we will be able to focus closely on the Resurrection.

In the first verse we read: ﴾Has there not come over the human being a period when they were a thing not worth mentioning﴿?[23]

The atoms which make up a person's physical body were spread over various parts of the earth - within the drops of water in the rivers and the air that blew over the earth. The primary matters used in the creation of the first human being were spread over these vast regions, and humanity was lost among them and was not even worth mentioning.

Is the meaning of 'human being' in this verse, a specific person, or is it reference to humanity in general? Is it a specific reference to Prophet Adam ? The verse which follows tells us that the 'human being' has been created from a drop of sperm, and thus this is a clear indication that the correct answer is that the 'human being' in this verse refers to humanity in general. However, some scholars believe that the reference to the 'human being' in the first verse is that of Adam , while in the second verse, it refers to the offspring of Adam ; however, it is highly improbable for this meaning to exist given that these two verses come one after another.

Regarding the exegesis of the sentence 'they were not even a thing worth mentioning,' numerous opinions are cited. One belief states that when a person was just a mere drop of sperm, and after that a fetus, they were a thing not spoken about. However, after

---

[23] Is the word *'hal'* which has been mentioned in this verse in the meaning of *'qad'* - which is used in Arabic to indicate a sense of completion in the past tense and can be translated into English as "already," "indeed," or "certainly" and it can also be used to refer to a rhetorical and negating question. In this regard, there are many different opinions given, however the apparent reading of this verse gives us the understanding that it is indeed a rhetorical question, thus the meaning of this verse would be:

أَلَيْسَ قَدْ أَتَى عَلَى الْإِنْسَانِ حِينٌ مِنَ الدَّهْرِ لَمْ يَكُنْ شَيْئًا مَذْكُورًا؟!

> 'Has there not come a time upon the human being when they were a thing not worth mentioning!?'

traversing through various stages in the womb resulting in one's physical completion, then a person becomes something which is spoken about and mentioned.

Imām Muḥammad al-Bāqir said: "A person is, in the Knowledge of Allah, something aforementioned; however in the world of creation, they were not spoken about."[24]

In some commentaries of the Quran, it is mentioned that the meaning of the 'human being' in this verse are the scholars who, before gaining their knowledge, are not worthy of being mentioned, however after attaining knowledge, they are remembered - either during their lifetime or after their death.

Other scholars have stated that when ʿUmar ibn al-Khaṭṭāb heard this verse being recited by someone, he said: "O how I wish Adam had remained (in his pre-earthly existence) and had never been brought into creation, so his sons would never have been evaluated!"[25]

It is astonishing to hear such a comment, as in reality, a complaint like this is an attack on the creation of humanity and an insult to the Creator!

※ ※ ※

After the stage of the creation of humankind and them becoming something worthy of mentioning, we read: ❮Surely, We have created the human being from a small life-germ uniting (itself): We mean to try them, so We have made them hearing (and) seeing❯.

The word 'small life-germ' is the plural of '*masj*,' or it may be the plural of '*mashīj*,' and it means 'something mixed.'[26]

---

[24] *Tafsīr Majmaʿ al-Bayān*, Vol. 10, Pg. 406.
[25] Ibid.
[26] Please note that whereas the word 'sperm' has been mentioned in the singular, however its characteristic of 'mixed' has been mentioned in the plural, and this is because the sperm itself is made up of various things

The creation of the human being is from a mixed sperm (this may refer to the uniting of a man's sperm with a woman's egg) - just as has been mentioned in the traditions of the Ahlul Bayt ﷺ in which this process has been discussed in general terms.

This verse may also refer to the various traits and characteristics which are present in the sperm, like its genetic inheritance from the genes which it carries and other such things. It may also relate to the mixture of various things which make up the sperm as there are numerous substances in each drop of sperm. It could even refer to a combination of all these things - and this last meaning is more comprehensive and appropriate to accept as the interpretation of this word.

A final possibility exists which states that the word *'amshāj'* refers to the course of movement of the sperm inside of the womb.

The phrase: 'We wish to evaluate them,' refers to this new creation reaching the stage of a human being with responsibilities upon themselves, many duties to fulfill, and a test to undergo from Allah ﷻ. This is one of the greatest bounties of Allah ﷻ in that a person has been given this great status and found worthy of having responsibilities and duties to perform towards Him. Since it is not possible to fulfill a responsibility and be thoroughly tested without having an awareness about what the test is regarding, in the last part of this section under review, some of the ways which can be used to recognize this test, such as the power of sight and hearing which a human being has at one's disposal, have been mentioned.

Exegetes of the Quran have stated that the meaning of 'testing,' as seen in this verse, are the changes which a fetus goes through from its beginning as a drop of sperm until it becomes a fully developed human being. However, by keeping in mind the use of

---

and falls under the ruling of the plural. Scholars, such as al-Zamakhsharī in his work, *Al-Kashshāf*, have stated that the word *'amshāj'* is the singular form of the word, even though it is based on the pattern of the plural.

the phrase: 'We wish to assess them' and the term 'human being' which has been used, the first exegesis given is the most appropriate one.

Thus, from the wordings of this verse, we come to understand that the source of all realizations which a person benefits from are one's senses. In other words, the awareness which comes about through the five senses is the root through which everything is understood, and this is the opinion of many of the Muslim philosophers and the Greek philosophers, one being Aristotle.

Seeing as how the responsibility which a person has on their shoulders, and the test which one is put through requires an individual to possess knowledge and awareness to be able to take the examination, and that one also requires the tools to develop this knowledge, a person requires two other things - guidance and the freedom of choice. Therefore, in the next verse under review it has been mentioned that: ﴾Surely, We have guided them to the way: they may be thankful or unthankful﴿.[27]

The phrase: 'We have guided that person' which is used in this verse has an extremely broad meaning, and includes the ontological guidance, the primordial guidance, and the legislational guidance, even though in the context of this verse, it may only refer to the legislational form of guidance.

[27] According to most exegetists of the Quran, the words 'thankful' and 'unthankful,' are expressional words for the objective pronoun contained in 'We have guided them.' Another possibility exists which states that the predicate *'yakūnu'* may be assumed to be contained in the verse, however, is not expressly mentioned. This would render the verse to be interpreted as stating:

إِمَّا يَكُونُ شَاكِرًا وَإِمَّا يَكُونُ كَفُورًا

'One is either thankful or one is unthankful.'

An explanation of this form of guidance noted above is: Seeing as how Allah ﷻ created humankind to test them and for them to reach perfection, the introductory steps to reach this goal have also been created within them, and the necessary powers to complete this test have also been granted to them - this is referred to as ontological guidance.

Following this stage, we see that deep within a person’s primordial nature, Allah ﷻ placed the love of traversing the path towards Him, and through the natural inspirations given to them, this path has also been shown. It is through this primordial guidance given to each human being that one makes the way to yet another path which is the Divinely-sent leaders and great Prophets - those who have been granted the teachings and clear rules and regulations directly from Allah ﷻ to show everyone the path towards the legislational guidance. Indeed, these three forms of guidance are universal and are for the benefit of all of humanity.

In summary, this verse points to three particularly important and determining issues in every person’s life:

1. Responsibilities.
2. Guidance.
3. Freedom of choice.

Each one of these correlate and complements one another. In addition, the verse which reads: ﴾Surely, We have shown them the way: they may be thankful or unthankful﴿ invalidates the beliefs of compulsion or coercion in one’s actions.

The use of the words ‘thankful’ and ‘unthankful’ are the most appropriate words which can be used in this instance because in the face of Divine blessings which is guidance to the path, a person who has been receptive and submissive, and has chosen the path of guidance will naturally be thankful for this great blessing. However, those who go against guidance are truly unthankful for what they have been granted!

Since not a single person's hands or tongue can ever truly thank Allah ﷻ as He deserves to be thanked, in this verse, the thanking Allah ﷻ has been mentioned as the active participle, whereas for the ungratefulness the word meaning extremely ungrateful has been used in the exaggerative form. This is because those who ignore this great bounty of Allah ﷻ - that is, the guidance - have committed the highest degree of ungratefulness since Allah ﷻ has provided them with all the various tools of guidance, and thus it is very ungrateful to ignore the bounty of guidance and take the wrong path in life.

Further to this, it must be noted that 'unthankful' is a word used both in the meaning of 'the denial of bounties,' and in relation to 'disbelief' regarding the theological issues, just as Rāghib has mentioned in his work, *Al-Mufradāt.*

In the last verse under review in this section, there is a brief, yet meaningful allusion to the eventual outcome of those who choose to take a path of disbelief and ingratitude: ﴾Surely, We have prepared for the unbelievers chains and shackles, and a burning fire﴿.

The use of the word 'We have prepared' is yet another emphasis on the fact that the punishment is something which will overcome a specific group of people, i.e., the disbelievers and unthankful people.

One reason that a person may prepare something beforehand which may not be used for some time is because one fears that later, they may be faced with a situation of limited ability to perform that task, thus when they need that thing, they will not be able to do it, so one 'keeps that ready' on hand. However, this definition has no meaning when it comes to Allah ﷻ since whatever He wishes to do, He merely needs to give the order of 'be' and it is immediately enacted! At the same time, to categorically state that this punishment will engulf the disbelievers, it is stated that the tools needed to punish them are already in existence!

The word 'chains' *(salāsil)* is the plural of *'silsilah,'* while the word 'shackles' *(aghlāl)* is the plural of *'ghill'* and means 'a loop or something spiral in shape which is placed around the neck or hands of a person,' like handcuffs, and then this thing is tied with chains.[28] The purpose of mentioning the words 'shackles' and 'chains' and the 'burning flames of fire' is to explain the great punishment which will be given to these people. This has also been mentioned in other verses of the Quran where the words 'punishment' and 'captivity' are mentioned in the plural.

These peoples' freedom about their desires of this transient world will lead to their captivity in the next world. It is the fire of this world which they paid no attention to which will manifest itself in the next world and engulf them.

Tumultuous World of the Fetus

We now know that a human fetus comes into existence by the union of a man's sperm with a woman's egg. The creation of the fetus, its composition, and then the various stages which the embryo goes through is one of the most amazing realities and wonders of the great world of creation that we are in. With all the advancements in the Science of Embryology, many curtains of the mysteries of this world have been lifted, however, certain other mysteries remain hidden. Some of the amazing facts which we allude to below make up only a small part of this entire process of life.

---

[28] For a deeper explanation regarding the meaning of *'aghlāl,'* refer to verse 8 of Sūrah Yāsīn, Vol. 18, Pg. 321 of *Tafsīr Nemunah.*

1. The semen which a man ejaculates are composed of sperms that are living, moving, microscopic organisms, each of which have a head, a neck, and a moving tail. It is interesting to note that with every ejaculation, anywhere from 200 to 500,000,000 sperms are released - a number which equals the population of many countries combined! However, from this uncountable number, only one or a few of them enter the woman's fallopian tubes and can fertilize an egg. The reason why such many sperm come out is because as the sperms travel to reach towards the egg and seek to join it, many of them end up dying, and if this vast number of sperm did not come out at the time of ejaculation, then it would have been difficult for an egg to ever be fertilized.

2. The womb of a woman, before the period of pregnancy, is about the size of a walnut, however after the egg is fertilized and the fetus begins to grow, it becomes so large that it ends up taking up a generous portion inside of the woman. It is amazing to see that the walls of the womb are so flexible and strong that even with such a heavy weight inside of it, it still can have such resilience!

3. The blood which lines the woman's womb is not from her blood veins; rather, it is moving in-between the various organs! If this blood were in the veins, then undoubtedly, with the potent force of the growing fetus pushing up against the walls of the woman, it could easily break!

4. Some researchers believe that the egg of a woman contains positive electricity, while the sperm has negative electricity within it, and it is for this reason that they are attracted to one another. When a sperm unites with an egg, it releases an electrical charge, and thus the countless other sperms which are around the one which entered the egg are expelled from that area! Other researchers state that when a sperm enters the egg, a chemical substance is excreted which forces the other sperms to flee!

5. The fetus lies within a large sack submerged in a thick, dark liquid called the amniotic fluid. This sack insulates the fetus against any rapid movements of the mother or hits on her abdomen.

Moreover, it keeps the fetus consistently warm such that the change of the outside temperature does not impact the temperature of the fetus. Most interestingly is that this large sack and the amniotic fluid puts the fetus into a weight-less environment and prevents the distinct parts of the fetus from exerting pressure on itself which may cause damage to it.

6. The food of the fetus comes from the placenta through the umbilical cord - meaning that the blood which flows through the mother contains the food and oxygen needed by the fetus, and this enters the placenta; then after going through another purification, it enters the heart of the fetus through the umbilical cord, and from there, that which the fetus needs is distributed throughout its entire body.

It is also interesting to note that the left and right side of the heart of the fetus are connected to one another since the filtration which is normally conducted by the lungs is not an issue for the fetus because the fetus does not breathe in the womb. However, upon birth, the chest cavity of the newborn separates, and the lungs begin to work and help the baby to breathe![29]

---

[29] Information for the data mentioned in this section has been taken from Volume 1 of the work, *The First University and the Last Prophet*, and other books.

Section Two - Verses 5 to 11

﴿إِنَّ ٱلْأَبْرَارَ يَشْرَبُونَ مِن كَأْسٍ كَانَ مِزَاجُهَا كَافُورًا ۝٥ عَيْنًا يَشْرَبُ بِهَا
عِبَادُ ٱللَّهِ يُفَجِّرُونَهَا تَفْجِيرًا ۝٦ يُوفُونَ بِٱلنَّذْرِ وَيَخَافُونَ يَوْمًا كَانَ شَرُّهُۥ
مُسْتَطِيرًا ۝٧ وَيُطْعِمُونَ ٱلطَّعَامَ عَلَىٰ حُبِّهِۦ مِسْكِينًا وَيَتِيمًا وَأَسِيرًا ۝٨ إِنَّمَا
نُطْعِمُكُمْ لِوَجْهِ ٱللَّهِ لَا نُرِيدُ مِنكُمْ جَزَآءً وَلَا شُكُورًا ۝٩ إِنَّا نَخَافُ مِن
رَّبِّنَا يَوْمًا عَبُوسًا قَمْطَرِيرًا ۝١٠ فَوَقَىٰهُمُ ٱللَّهُ شَرَّ ذَٰلِكَ ٱلْيَوْمِ وَلَقَّىٰهُمْ نَضْرَةً
وَسُرُورًا ۝١١﴾

"Surely, the righteous shall drink from a cup the admixture of which is camphor. ۝ A fountain from which the servants of Allah will drink; they make it to flow a (goodly) flowing forth. ۝ They fulfill the vows and fear a day the evil of which shall spread everywhere. ۝ And they give food out of love for Him to the poor, the orphan, and the captive. ۝ We only feed you for Allah's sake; we desire from you neither reward, nor thanks. ۝ Surely, we fear from our Lord a stern, distressful day. ۝ Therefore, Allah will guard them from the evil of that day and cause them to meet (Him) with ease and happiness."

Status of the Ahlul Bayt عليهم السلام

Ibn ʿAbbās narrates: "Both Ḥasan and Ḥusayn were sick when the Prophet, along with a group of his companions, came to see how they were doing.

The Prophet said to Imām ʿAlī: 'O Abūl Ḥasan! It would be good if you took an oath (to Allah) for your children to be cured from their sickness.'

Thus, Imām ʿAlī, Fāṭima, and their female-servant, Fiḍḍah, made an oath to Allah that if the children recover, then they will fast for three days - and according to some traditions, Ḥasan and Ḥusayn also took part in the oath that they too would fast for three days [when they get better].

A brief time elapsed and both were cured from their sickness.

Even though they had very little food in the house, Imām ʿAlī still divided the barely he had at home into three portions, and his wife, Fāṭima, took one-third of this and ground it into flour and baked bread with it.

At the time of breaking their fast, a beggar came to the door of their house and said: 'Peace be upon you, O family of Muḥammad! I am a poor person from among the poor Muslims. Please give me some food - may Allah bless you with food from Paradise!'

All the members of the house placed this poor person's needs ahead of their own, and each of them gave their portion of bread to the poor man, and that evening, they all broke their fast with only water.

On the second day, they again kept a fast, and at the time of breaking the fast with the food which had been prepared (barley bread), an orphan came to the door, and just like the previous day, they all gave the orphan whatever they had. Again, they broke their fast with only water, and prepared to begin the third day of fasting.

On the third day, a war-captive (prisoner) came to their house at sunset, asking for food, and once again, this family gave away all the food which they had!

When the morning of the fourth day came, Imām ʿAlī took Ḥasan and Ḥusayn by the hand and went to see the Prophet. When the Prophet set eyes upon them, he saw them trembling due to their intense hunger! He immediately said to them: 'It is very troubling for me to see you in such a state!' The Prophet got up and accompanied them to the house of Fāṭima and saw her standing in the prayer niche. She too was suffering the pangs of hunger which were evident from her frail body and the heavy inset of her eyes. Witnessing this heart-breaking sight, the Prophet became extremely grieved.

Immediately at this point, Angel Jibrā'īl came down and said: 'O Muḥammad! Take this chapter (of the Quran)! Allah sends His salutations upon such a family.'

The Prophet then recited the chapter which was revealed to him: "Sūrah Hal Atā." [According to some scholars, the Prophet recited from "...surely the righteous..." until "...surely your endeavours shall be thanked..." which makes up eighteen verses which were revealed to him]."

The incident narrated above is a summarized version of the tradition as mentioned in the book, *Al-Ghadīr* by ʿAllāmāh Amīnī.

This narration is like numerous other traditions found in other books which have been stated regarding this event. In *Al-Ghadīr*, there are traditions from thirty-four well-known scholars of the Ahl al-Sunnah who have narrated this tradition in their books, and ʿAllāmāh Amīnī mentions the names of these books and the pages on which this information can be found. Thus, the tradition quoted above is very famous among the scholars of the Ahl al-Sunnah. In fact, it is a consecutively narrated tradition (*mutawātir*).[30]

Shīʿa scholars are unanimous that these eighteen verses, or rather the entire chapter, was revealed regarding the noted event, and all of them without exception have stated in the books of exegesis and traditions that the narrations about this event constitute one of the important distinctions and virtues of Imām ʿAlī ☙, Lady Fāṭima al-Zahrā' ☙, their two sons, and their servant Fiḍḍah.

In addition, just as we mentioned in the beginning of this Sūrah, this event is so well-known and acknowledged that even in the

---

[30] Refer to *Al-Ghadīr*, Vol. 3, Pp. 107 to 111; *Aḥqāq al-Ḥaqq*, Vol. 3, Pp. 157 to 171 in which the above quoted tradition has been narrated from 36 scholars and leaders of the Ahl al-Sunnah, including their sources of reference.

poems which have been written by both the Shīʿa and Ahl al-Sunnah, such as the famous poem of Imām al-Shāfiʿī, this event has been mentioned!

At this point, let us review some of the excuses that are brought up every time the merits and greatness of Imām ʿAlī are brought forth by those who show an extreme sense of resentment towards him.

Argument 1: They say that this chapter was revealed in Mecca, whereas the particular historical event clearly shows us that this chapter was revealed in regard to something which happened <u>after</u> the birth of Imām Ḥasan and Imām Ḥusayn - which no doubt took place in Medina.

Reply: As we touched on briefly at the beginning of this chapter, we have clear proofs in hand which show that the entire content of Sūrah Hal Atā, or at least the eighteen verses mentioned previously, were revealed in Medina.

Argument 2: The wordings of the verses are of a general nature, so how can we apply them to specific individuals?

Reply: It is understood that simply having verses which are of a general nature does not go against the principle that they may be revealed for specific individuals. There are many verses of the Quran which have a very general and comprehensive meaning; however, the history of revelation shows us that they have a specific interpretation. It is amazing to see that some people can take a general understanding of a verse to negate the history of revelation of that specific verse!

Argument 3: Some individuals have stated that there are other reasons for the revelation of this chapter and its verses, and these reasons are not in line with what has been stated. One of these people include al-Suyūṭī in his work, *Durr al-Manthūr*, who has narrated that an African man came to the Prophet and asked him about the glorification and praise of Allah. ʿUmar stood up and told the man: "You have asked the Messenger of Allah enough questions!" To this, the Prophet replied: "Be quiet ʿUmar!" It was at this time that the chapter of Hal Atā was sent down to the Prophet ﷺ![31]

In another tradition mentioned in *Durr al-Manthūr*, it has been stated that a man from Ethiopia came to the Messenger of Allah ﷺ and wanted to ask him a question.

The Prophet ﷺ told him to go ahead and ask him, then wait for his reply.

The man asked: "O Messenger of Allah! A group of you (Muslims), from the point of view of your skin colour, facial characteristics, and status, have a greater rank than we do. If I too bring about true faith in what you all believe and I act in the same way that you act (performing righteous deeds), then will I be in Paradise with you?" The Prophet ﷺ replied: "Yes. I swear by the One who holds my life in His hands that the trail of (spiritual) light of the black-skinned people will be seen in Paradise for the span of 1,000 years."

At this point, the Prophet ﷺ went on to explain the great rewards given to a person who says: "There is no entity worthy of worship except for Allah, and Glory and Praise be to Allah," and it was at this time that Sūrah Hal Atā was revealed.[32]

Reply: Keeping in mind that these traditions have pretty much no correlation to the contents of Sūrah Hal Atā, such traditions were fabricated by the Umayyad Dynasty or others to crush the true history of revelation of this chapter!

Argument 4: Another excuse may be given regarding the actual history of revelation of this chapter, and one may ask how is it possible for a person to go three days without food and to break one's fast with merely a glass of water!?

Reply: This is one of the most ridiculous criticisms that can be brought up in regard to this chapter as we ourselves have seen many people in our lifetime who in order to be cured of a specific

---

[31] *Tafsīr Durr al-Manthūr*, Vol. 6, Pg. 297.

[32] Ibid.

sickness, have been instructed by their doctor to fast for not only three days which is quite easy, but rather they have fasted for a period of forty days in which they only drink water and completely abstain from food! It is through such a medically sanctioned program that they have been able to ward off many illnesses!

In addition, a well-known, non-Muslim doctor named Alexi Soforin has authored a book regarding the medicinal benefits of such a fast and has even mentioned a very precise program to follow in this regard.[33]

Argument 5: There are others who, to disregard the greatness (of the family of the Prophet ﷺ) that is seen in this chapter, have taken another route, and state other things such as the following:

A scholar of the Ahl al-Sunnah, al-Ālūsī, wrote: "Even if we were to say that this chapter was not revealed regarding Imām ʿAlī and Fāṭima, then this does not remove anything from their worth and status since them being referred to as 'righteous individuals' (in other narrations) is well-known to everyone."

He then goes on to list some of their virtues and states: "What can anyone say in regard to these two individuals except that Imām ʿAlī is the master of all the true believers and the executor *(waṣī)* of the will of the Prophet; and Fāṭima is a part of the body of the Messenger of Allah and is considered a share-holder of the essence of Muḥammadī; and Ḥasanayn are the spirit and essence and the leaders of the youths of Paradise!? However, what we have just stated does not mean that we renounce others (around the Prophet), rather we state that anyone who does not follow their path is indeed misguided."[34]

Reply: We state that if such a great worth and honour which is so well-known (throughout the Islamic texts) is neglected and passed over, then slowly other virtues will also meet the same fate

---

[33] Some of the information from this Russian author can be found at http://tasbeha.org/content/hh_books/fasting/index.html. (Tr.)

[34] *Tafsīr Rūḥ al-Maʿānī*, Vol. 29, Pg. 158.

and a day will come when some of the main merits of Imām ʿAlī, Lady Fāṭima al-Zahrāʾ, and Ḥasanayn will also be denied!

It must be noted that in some traditions which have been narrated directly from Imām ʿAlī, he used these verses in various debates with his opponents to show the status of his two sons and himself.[35]

Further to the above points, it is important to mention that a 'war captive' was a term normally used in Medina since in Mecca, due to the fact that no Islamically permitted wars had taken place, this term was not used much, if even at all - and this is another proof of this chapter being revealed in Medina.

The final point which we must mention is that according to the opinion of a group of scholars, such as al-Ālūsī, the well-known commentator of the Ahl al-Sunnah, many of the pleasures and bounties of Paradise have been mentioned in this chapter, except for the *Ḥūr al-ʿAyn*[36] which in the Noble Quran are most often considered as one of the pleasures of Paradise - however, in this chapter, there is absolutely no mention of them! It is possible that this may be since this chapter was revealed about Lady Fāṭima al-Zahrāʾ, her husband, and their two sons, and due to the respect

---

[35] Refer to *Al-Iḥtijāj* of Shaykh Ṭabrisī and *Al-Khiṣāl* of Shaykh Ṣadūq, as has been quoted in *Al-Mizān fī Tafsīr al-Quran*, Vol. 20, Pg. 224.

[36] *Ḥūr al-ʿAyn* is a term in Islamic eschatology (the study of the end times) that is often mentioned in the context of Paradise or the afterlife in Islam. It is used to describe beautiful and pure maidens or heavenly beings in Paradise who are said to be a reward for righteous believers, particularly in the context of martyrdom. In Islamic tradition, it is believed that those who lead a pious life and are granted entry into Paradise will be rewarded with various pleasures and blessings, and *Ḥūr al-ʿAyn* is often mentioned as one of these rewards. These beings are described as exceptionally beautiful and pure, created specifically to provide companionship and delight to the righteous inhabitants of Paradise.

being shown to this great woman of Islam, there is **no** mention whatsoever about the *Ḥūr al-'Ayn*![37]

Our discussion about the history of revelation of this section was quite long, however we had no choice but to explain this issue in detail given the unfair accusations which have been leveled regarding its revelation.

Great Reward for the Righteous

In the previous verses, after humankind was divided into two categories - 'the thankful' and 'the unthankful or ungrateful;' also known as 'those who express gratitude for what they are given' and 'those who are not in the least appreciative of the bounties they have been given,' we are presented with a short glimpse of the painful punishment that has been prepared for the ungrateful ones. However, the verses under review also explain the rewards of the thankful and righteous good doers and spiritually-purified ones, and indeed some interesting points are mentioned.

First off, it says: ﴾Surely, the righteous shall drink from a cup, the admixture of which is camphor﴿.

The word 'righteous' *(abrār)* is the plural of *'birr,'* and its original meaning is 'something very wide,' and it is for this reason that a wide and open expanse of desert is known as *'barr'* with a '*fatha*' on the first letter. Since a person's righteous actions have a wide-reaching outcome within society, it is for this reason that this word has come to be used for such an individual. However, the word *'birr'* with a '*kasrah*' on the first letter refers to 'a person who does good.' Some scholars have stated that there is a difference between 'righteous' and 'goodness' and that is the former refers to an act of goodness which is done with complete understanding,

[37] *Tafsīr Rūḥ al-Ma'ānī*, Vol. 29, Pg. 158.

while the latter is a general word for any act of goodness that is done without any understanding of its merits.

The word *'kāfūr'* has many meanings from the lexical point of view, but the most well-known one is a 'good smelling thing' such as sweet-smelling plants. Another meaning of this word is camphor which has a strong and powerful smell and is known as a disinfectant.

The above-mentioned verse shows us that this pure drink of Paradise will be something which has a strong aroma and is not something that only the tastebuds will experience, but even the smell will reach the (nose) glands!

Some exegetes of the Quran state that *'kāfūr'* or 'camphor' in this verse is the name of a spring of Paradise, however this interpretation does not fit with the reading of the verse: ﴾...the admixture of which is camphor﴿.

Since the word *'kāfūr'* comes from the root *'ka-fa-ra'* which means 'to cover something,' some scholars of the ʿArabic language, such as al-Rāghib in *Al-Mufradāt*, believe that this word was chosen for 'camphor' because the part of the tree from which this substance is extracted is hidden from one's sight - under the bark of the tree. Other scholars have stated that the word *'kāfūr'* or 'camphor' refers to an extremely white and cool substance because usually camphor brings coolness to the one who uses it, and its extreme whiteness is something which is often used in similitudes.

Keeping in mind what we have stated, the first exegesis given is the correct one, especially since sometimes in the Islamic texts, the word camphor has been used alongside musk and amber which are some of the best forms of perfume.

The source of this glass of pure drink is then mentioned: ❮A fountain from which the servants of Allah will drink; they make it to flow a (goodly) flowing forth (from wherever they wish❯.[38 & 39]

The source of this pure drink which will be placed at the disposal of the righteous individuals and servants of Allah ﷻ will be done in such a way that wherever they are and whenever they wish to drink from it, it will be ready for them! Regarding the starting place and spring of this drink, Imām Muḥammad al-Bāqir ؑ stated:

هِيَ عَيْنٌ فِي دَارِ النَّبِـيِّ تُفَجِّرُ إِلَى دَوْرِ الْأَنْبِيَاءِ وَ الْمُؤْمِنِينَ.

"This is a spring which starts from the house of the Prophet and goes through the houses of (all the other) Prophets and the true believers."[40]

---

[38] One may wonder why is the word *'ayna'* or 'spring' in this verse in the accusative (this case is marked by a fatḥa or a dash above the word making a short "a" sound) form? There are some strong possibilities mentioned by the scholars. Perhaps the most appropriate of these is to state that the word *'ayna'* is in a state of being in the accusative due to the rule in 'Arabic grammar of removal, and it can be presumed that the phrase *'min 'ayna'* or '(from a spring)' is the actual meaning. Some other scholars have stated that the rule of something which stands in the place of something else is at play here, which in this case is the word *'kāfūr'* or 'camphor;' or that it is in the accusative state due to it being regarded as a word denoting specification or extending praise. It is also possible that it refers to the passive participle, which is not expressly mentioned, however is taken as being understood, and thus can be understood as being *'yashrabūn 'ayn'* or '(drinking (from a) spring of water),' however just as was previously stated, the first opinion given is more appropriate.

[39] The word 'they will drink' can become transitive through the letter *'bā'* or even without it, and it is possible that as it has been mentioned in the word *'bihā'* it would be in the meaning of 'from.'

[40] *Tafsīr Nūr al-Thaqalayn*, Vol. 5, Pg. 477; *Tafsīr Rūḥ al-Maʿānī*, Vol. 29, Pg. 155.

Just like in the life of this world in which the sources of knowledge and mercy flow from the house of the Noble Prophet ﷺ towards the servants of Allah ﷻ and the righteous doers, in the next life, which will be a greater manifestation of this similitude, the well of this pure drink of the Divine will also begin from the house of revelation, and the streams from this well will flow into the houses of the true believers!

The word for 'flowing forth' which is *'yufajjiru'* comes the root word *'fa-ja-ra'* whose original meaning was to 'split something large' - whether this be the splitting of the ground or something else. Since the morning light breaks open the curtains of the night, the morning time is referred to as *'fajr.'* In addition, a person who is an open sinner and transgressor is referred to as a *'fājir'* since they rip open the veils of modesty and spiritual purity and choose to leave the path of the truth. However, in the verse under review, the meaning of this word is the 'splitting of the ground.'

It should be noted that among all the bounties of Paradise which have been mentioned in this chapter, the first one is that of a pure and aromatic drink. This may be since after completing the accounting for one's deeds on the plain of *Maḥshar* - the area in which all of humanity will gather for their deeds to be accounted for, a person will then step into Paradise and drink from this elixir which will remove all their grief and sorrow! From here, with a presence that is completely spiritually intoxicated with the love of Allah ﷻ, one will then be able to partake in the other Divine gifts that are waiting for them in Paradise.

After discussing the actions and characteristics of the righteous people and the servants of Allah ﷻ, we are then given five reasons why these people deserve all these incomparable bounties.

We first read: ﴾They fulfill the vows, and they fear a day the evil of which will be spreading far and wide﴿.

The words 'they fulfill' and 'they fear' and the sentences which come after this are all in the present/future verbal form tense, and this shows that this is a lifetime program which is perpetual. However, like it was stated in the history of revelation of these verses, the true and perfect manifestation of these events is Imām ʿAlī ﷺ, Lady Fāṭima al-Zahrā᾽ ﷺ, and their two sons, Ḥasan ﷺ and Ḥusayn ﷺ, who fulfilled the oath that they had made and fasted for three consecutive days, breaking their fast with a mere glass of water! It was through this action of theirs that their hearts became even more so filled with the awe of Allah ﷻ and the anxiety over the Day of Judgement.

The word *'musṭatīr'* means 'expansive' and 'far-flung' and points to the various forms of punishment which will take place on that grand day.

When such individuals fulfill the vows that they made obligatory upon themselves, they have lived up to and given the rights to the obligatory acts of the Divine in the most perfect way, as they struggle to ensure the performance of such vows. The fear of these people for the consequences of that momentous Day is a reference to their faith in the Day of Accounting, and their feelings of an intense responsibility which lies on their shoulders regarding the fulfillment of the commandments of Allah ﷻ.

These personalities have a strong belief in the Resurrection and possess complete faith in all forms of punishment for the evil doers, and this is reflected in their actions.

۞ ۞ ۞

At this point, the third righteous deed is mentioned: ﴾And they give food out of love for Him to the poor, the orphan, and the captive﴿.

It is not an easy task to feed these sorts of people - rather it takes self-sacrifice of the highest level to perform such an action - especially when the person themselves are in a state of desperate need! From another point of view, the food is being fed to people of various backgrounds, thus one needs to be able to tolerate such people - the poor, the orphans, and the war captives. The extreme mercy which the members of the Ahlul Bayt ﷺ have for others is universal, and their assistance and support includes everyone.

The pronoun in the phrase *'alā ḥubbihi'* which means 'out of love for Him' returns to 'food' - meaning that even though they had a love and longing for the food due to their fasting, they still gave it up for the love of Allah ﷻ.

This is the same thing that can be seen in verse 92 of Sūrah Āle 'Imrān (3) which states:

﴿ لَنْ تَنَالُوا الْبِرَّ حَتَّىٰ تُنْفِقُوا مِمَّا تُحِبُّونَ ﴾

> "Never shall you attain righteousness until you spend out of that which you love."

Other scholars have stated that the pronoun in the phrase *'alā ḥubbihi'* returns to Allah ﷻ which was mentioned in the previous verse, so in this scenario, the verse would mean: "They give their food to the poor, the orphan, and the war captive only for the love and sake of Allah."

However, keeping in mind that this comes up in the next verse, the first opinion given is the more correct one in our opinion.

The meaning of 'a poor person,' 'an orphan,' and 'a war captive' are clear terms, however, what is the detailed meaning of the term 'war captive' - who does this allude to and what kind of a war captive were they? This is a point of discussion among the commentators of the Quran.

Many exegetes have stated that the 'war captive' could have been from the polytheists or disbelievers who came to seek assistance under the protection of the Islamic government in Medina. Some scholars have stated that the meaning of 'war captive' in this verse was a slave who was owned by a person and needed help. Yet other scholars have stated that the meaning of 'war captive' was a prisoner. However, the first interpretation is the most appropriate and accepted one.

At this point, another question arises: According to the history of revelation of this verse, a war captive came to the house of Imām ʿAlī ؑ at the time of breaking the fast, but were war captives not held in a prison cell?

The answer to this question will become clear by keeping in mind the following point:

According to historical narrations, during the time of the Prophet ﷺ, there were absolutely no prisoners of war. It was the Prophet ﷺ himself who would distribute the prisoners to other Muslims for them to maintain and look after. The Prophet ﷺ told the Muslims that they must watch over these people and treat them with kindness. Sometimes, it so happened that the Muslims did not have the ability to feed themselves, let alone their prisoners, and thus they would seek assistance from other Muslims to help feed them. Often, these prisoners would go along with the Muslims who were guarding them, while at other times, they would be instructed to go out on their own to other Muslims to seek food and assistance. As we know, at that time in history, the Muslims were under numerous pressures and difficulties, thus food and other necessities were very scarce.

Of course, after some time when the Islamic government spread and established itself, the number of prisoners also increased, and the number of criminals was also on the increase throughout the Islamic lands. It was at this time that 'formal prisons' took shape, and the feeding and taking care of these prisoners was then conducted through the public treasury of the government.[41]

Therefore, from the above-mentioned verse, we can clearly deduce that one of the best actions is to feed the needy and destitute - not only the needy Muslims who are held captive in jails

---

[41] For a detailed explanation on this issue, please refer to the book, *Rulings for Prisons in Islam*.

in non-Islamic countries; but in addition, even the non-Muslims fall under this Islamic ruling. We see that feeding one such individual is considered as one of the greatest acts of the righteous individuals!

In a tradition from the Messenger of Allah ﷺ, we read that:

إِسْتَوْصُوا بِالأَسْرىٰ خَيْرًا وَكَانَ أَحَدُهُمْ يُؤْثِرُ أَسِيرَهُ بِطَعَامِهِ.

"Deal with the prisoners in the best of ways and prefer them (the prisoners) over your own selves by even giving them your food."[42]

The fourth noble action of these righteous individuals was their true sincerity because they said: ﴾We feed you only for Allah's sake; we desire from you neither reward, nor thanks﴿.

This program of life is not limited to merely feeding others, rather, it is one in which all the deeds of a person are done with purity of the heart and solely for the sake of Allah ﷻ, in which there is not even the slightest hope of receiving a reward from any people, in fact, they do not even ask for praise or thanks!

Principally, we see that in Islam, the worth of an action is based on the sincerity of the intention behind that act, and if any action is performed with an intention of being for other than Allah ﷻ - whether it is for showing off, for one's own lower self or ego, for the praise and thanks from people, or for a material reward in this life, then such an action will have absolutely no spiritual or Divine reward.

In a famous tradition from the Noble Prophet of Islam ﷺ, we read:

لاَ عَمَلٌ إِلَّا بِالنِّيَّةِ وَإِنَّمَا الْأَعْمَالُ بِالنِّيَّاتِ.

---

[42] Ibn Athīr, *Al-Kāmil*, Vol. 2, Pg. 131.

> "There is no action (that is accepted by Allah ﷻ) except with a (sincere) intention (attached to it), and surely all actions are based on their intentions."

Going to how the verse starts in which the Quran states that these people feed only for the sake of Allāh ﷻ - the 'face of Allah' is the sacred Essence of Allah ﷻ, since Allah ﷻ does not have a physical face. This also comes in the meaning of the pleasure of Allah ﷻ and has been emphasized in other verses of the Quran, such as in Sūrah al-Baqarah (2), verse 272:

﴿وَ مَا تُنْفِقُونَ إِلاَّ ابْتِغَاءَ وَجْهِ اللَّهِ﴾

> "...and you do not spend but to seek the pleasure of Allah..."

In addition, in Sūrah al-Kahf (18), verse 28, when describing the righteous companions of the Prophet ﷺ, we read that:

﴿وَاصْبِرْ نَفْسَكَ مَعَ الَّذِينَ يَدْعُونَ رَبَّهُمْ بِالْغَدَاةِ وَالْعَشِيِّ يُرِيدُونَ وَجْهَهُ﴾

> "And keep yourself patient (by being) with those who call on their Lord morning and evening, desiring His pleasure (goodwill)..."

In the final verse which describes the actions of these righteous individuals we read: ﴾Surely, we fear from our Lord a stern, distressful Day﴿.

It is possible that these words were not verbally spoken, but rather through their demeanour and actions, they were understood; and it is also possible that these individuals verbally uttered such statements.

It should be noted that the word 'stern and distressful' has been used for the Day of Judgement, but this word is usually only used as a characteristic for a human being and refers to a person who is rude and crass. However, in this verse, we see it used for a non-living being, and this is because it is an emphasis on the fearful state of that Day. By this we mean that the Day of Resurrection will be so difficult and frightful that not only will humankind be in a state of distress, but rather, even that day itself will be one of distress! Furthermore, it can be stated that the day itself will feel distress, just like a human is scared!

What is the meaning of the word *'qamṭarīr'* and from what root word does this originate? The exegetes of the Quran and the scholars of the ʿArabic language have discussed this issue at length. Some scholars state that this word comes from *'qamṭar,'* while others have stated that it is derived from *'qaṭar'* and the *'mīm'* has been added to it. However, the most prominent opinion is the first one given, and thus this word means 'a great sense of distress and fright.'[43]

At this point, a question may come up that: If the righteous people are working solely for the sake of Allah ﷻ, then why should they say that they are fearful of the punishment of that Day? Is the motivation of working for Allah ﷻ conducive to working due to the fear of the punishment of the Resurrection!?

If we keep in mind the following point, then the answer to this question will become clear to us:

Even though these people are working solely for Allah ﷻ, they fear the punishment of the next life because this is a punishment from Allah ﷻ; if they have an affinity to the pleasures of Paradise then they do so because these blessings and pleasures stem from Him as well. This is the same thing which is mentioned in the books of Jurisprudence in the section on intention of the acts of worship where we read: "Having the intention of closeness to

---

[43] Rāghib al-Iṣfahānī, *Al-Mufradāt*; Ibn Manzūr, *Lisān al-ʿArab*; *al-Munjid*; Muḥammad ibn Aḥmad ibn Abī Bakr al-Anṣārī al-Qurṭubī, *Tafsīr al-Qurṭubī*, and Aḥmad ibn Abī Ṭālib al-Ṭabarsī, *Tafsīr Majmaʿ al-Bayān*.

Allah ﷻ in our actions of worship does not go against the motivation of the attraction for the reward, or the fear of the punishment, or even the granting of Divine material gifts while in this transient world from Allah ﷻ - such as a person performing the special *ṣalāt* for rain - *Ṣalāt al-Istisqā᾿* - since all of these things return back to Allah ﷻ. In addition, this is something which is referred to as a "motivation for a motivation" even though the highest stage of worship is one in which there is no motivation of an action due to desire for the pleasures of Paradise, or the fear of the punishment of the Hellfire, rather, everything is done under the guise of the love of Allah ﷻ."

In addition, the phrase: ﴾We fear from our Lord a stern, distressful Day﴿ also alludes to the fact that this fear is also a fear of Allah ﷻ.

A point which is interesting to note is that the second and fifth characteristics are both about fear with the difference that in the first scenario, there is only talk about the **fear of the Day of Judgement**, while in the second instance, there is mention about the **fear of Allah ﷻ on the Day of Judgement**.

In one verse, the Day of Resurrection has been presented such that the fear of that Day will be widespread; while in another instance, in the fifth characteristic, there is talk about the fright and extreme terror, which shows the vastness of that Day, and the vastness of the punishments and fears as well.

In the last verse under review, verse 11, we reach the general conclusion of the righteous actions and pure intentions which these noble individuals had and are told: ﴾Therefore, Allah will guard them from the evil of that Day and will cause them to meet with ease and happiness﴿.

The word 'ease' means cheerfulness, opulence, and a particular form of tenderness which will come about due to the superabundance of blessings and pleasures given to a person. The look of tranquility, inner peace, and happiness on the faces of these individuals will be apparent for everyone to see! Thus, if while in the transient world, these individuals felt a sense of responsibility about that fearful Day, then in exchange, Allah ﷻ will drown them in delight and pleasures on that Day.

The use of the word 'shall cause them to meet' is one of the most interesting terms used which shows that Allah ﷻ will welcome His guests with a special form of kindness and will drown them in pleasures and happiness in the shadow of His Mercy.

Feeding the Hungry

Not only in the verses under discussion is the topic of feeding people considered as one of the noble deeds for the righteous and true servants of Allah ﷻ, rather this has also been emphasized in many other verses of the Quran, and it shows that Allah ﷻ has a special affinity with this action.

When we look at the world today and examine the published news reports, we read that every year millions of people die from hunger; whereas in other parts of the world, there is such an excess of food, that they end up throwing away so much that one cannot even begin to calculate how much is wasted! When we weigh the importance of this Islamic commandment and look at the state of the world in which we are living, we see the worth of such noble ethical teachings of Islam.

There is also great emphasis in the Islamic narrations on this action which we can better understand in the light of the following traditions:

1. The Noble Prophet ﷺ stated that:

مَنْ أَطْعَمَ ثَلَاثَةَ نَفَرٍ مِنَ الْمُسْلِمِينَ أَطْعَمَهُ اللّٰهُ مِنْ ثَلَاثِ جِنَانٍ فِي مَلَكُوتِ السَّمٰوَاتِ.

"A person who feeds three Muslims will be fed by Allah from the food of three gardens of Paradise in the celestial heavens."[44]

2. Imām Jaʿfar al-Ṣādiq said:

مَنْ أَطْعَمَ مُؤْمِنًا حَتَّى يَشْبَعَهُ لَمْ يَدْرِ أَحَدٌ مِنْ خَلْقِ اللهِ مَا لَهُ مِنَ الْأَجْرِ فِي الآخِرَةِ، لاَ مَلَكٌ مُقَرَّبٌ، وَلاَ نَبِيٌّ مُرْسَلٌ إِلاَّ اللّٰهَ رَبَّ الْعَالَمِينَ.

"Not a single person from the creations of Allah can comprehend the reward (that will be) given in the next life to a person who feeds a believer until they are satiated - not the close angels to Allah, and not even the deputed Prophets - only Allah, the Lord of the Universe (can measure this reward)."[45]

3. In another tradition, also narrated to us from Imām Jaʿfar al-Ṣādiq we read:

لَإِنْ أَطْعَمَ مُؤْمِنًا مُحْتَاجًا أَحَبُّ إِلَيَّ مِنْ أَنْ أَزُورَهُ، وَلَإِنْ أَزُورَهُ أَحَبُّ إِلَيَّ مِنْ أَنْ أَعْتَقَ عَشْرَ رِقَابٍ.

"If I was to feed a needy believer, then this would be more beloved to me than going to visit them (which also has great rewards); and if I was to go and visit them, this is even more loved to me than freeing ten slaves!"[46]

Note that in such traditions, we are not only encouraged to feed the poor and hungry, rather in some narrations, it is clearly stated that feeding the believers - even if they are not needy - is equivalent to freeing a slave! This shows us that the act of feeding others is not only in place to alleviate the needs of the people, but

---

[44] *Al-Kāfī*, Vol. 2, Section on Feeding a Believer, Tradition 3.
[45] Ibid., Tradition 6.
[46] Ibid., Tradition 18.

it is also there to foster love, unity, friendship, and closeness with one another! The opposite can be seen in the materialistic world of today in which sometimes two close friends or relatives will go to a restaurant together, and each of them will pay their own portion of the bill. It is as if the act of being kind to one another is something strange to them!

In other traditions, it has been stated that feeding hungry people in general - even if they are not believers or Muslims - has been considered as one of the best actions, as can be seen in a tradition from the Noble Prophet of Islam ﷺ:

مِنْ أَفْضَلِ الْأَعْمَالِ عِنْدَ اللهِ إِبْرَادُ الْكِبَادِ الْحَارَّةِ وَإِشْبَاعُ الْكِبَادِ الْجَائِعَةِ وَالَّذِي نَفْسُ مُحَمَّدٍ بِيَدِهِ لاَ يُؤْمِنُ بِي عَبْدٌ يَبِيتُ شَبْعَانَ وَأَخُوهُ - أَوْ قَالَ جَارُهُ - الْمُسْلِمُ جَائِعٌ.

> "One of the best actions in the sight of Allah is to cool the burning livers [help alleviate a person's difficulties] and feed the hungry stomachs. I swear by the One who holds the soul of Muḥammad in His hands that a servant who goes to sleep while their brother in faith - or [in other readings of this *ḥadīth*] their neighbour - goes to bed hungry has not truly believed in me!"[47]

Although the above-mentioned tradition is in regard to feeding a Muslim, however we see in the beginning that it speaks about feeding any hungry person, thus it is not improbable to assume that it has a wide interpretation, and it may even include the

---

[47] *Biḥār al-Anwār*, Vol. 74, Pg. 369. It is important to note that the late ʿAllāmah Majlisī has presented an entire section which comprises 113 traditions regarding feeding and clothing a true believer. In addition, he has compiled traditions which speak about paying another person's debts; and some of the traditions mentioned in the chapter of his magnum opus are very general, and not specifically related to feeding or clothing a believer - rather any human being.

animals, for surely in this regard as well, there are numerous traditions.[48]

[48] *Biḥār al-Anwār*, Vol. 74, Pg. 369.

Section Three - Verses 12 to 22

﴿وَجَزَىٰهُم بِمَا صَبَرُواْ جَنَّةً وَحَرِيرًا ۝١٢ مُّتَّكِـِٔينَ فِيهَا عَلَى ٱلۡأَرَآئِكِۖ لَا يَرَوۡنَ
فِيهَا شَمۡسًا وَلَا زَمۡهَرِيرًا ۝١٣ وَدَانِيَةً عَلَيۡهِمۡ ظِلَٰلُهَا وَذُلِّلَتۡ قُطُوفُهَا تَذۡلِيلًا
۝١٤ وَيُطَافُ عَلَيۡهِم بِـَٔانِيَةٖ مِّن فِضَّةٖ وَأَكۡوَابٖ كَانَتۡ قَوَارِيرَا۠ ۝١٥ قَوَارِيرَاْ مِن
فِضَّةٖ قَدَّرُوهَا تَقۡدِيرًا ۝١٦ وَيُسۡقَوۡنَ فِيهَا كَأۡسٗا كَانَ مِزَاجُهَا زَنجَبِيلًا ۝١٧ عَيۡنٗا
فِيهَا تُسَمَّىٰ سَلۡسَبِيلٗا ۝١٨ وَيَطُوفُ عَلَيۡهِمۡ وِلۡدَٰنٞ مُّخَلَّدُونَ إِذَا رَأَيۡتَهُمۡ
حَسِبۡتَهُمۡ لُؤۡلُؤٗا مَّنثُورٗا ۝١٩ وَإِذَا رَأَيۡتَ ثَمَّ رَأَيۡتَ نَعِيمٗا وَمُلۡكٗا كَبِيرًا ۝٢٠
عَٰلِيَهُمۡ ثِيَابُ سُندُسٍ خُضۡرٞ وَإِسۡتَبۡرَقٞۖ وَحُلُّوٓاْ أَسَاوِرَ مِن فِضَّةٖ وَسَقَىٰهُمۡ رَبُّهُمۡ
شَرَابٗا طَهُورًا ۝٢١ إِنَّ هَٰذَا كَانَ لَكُمۡ جَزَآءٗ وَكَانَ سَعۡيُكُم مَّشۡكُورًا ۝٢٢﴾

"And reward them, because they were patient, with garden and silk, ۝ Reclining therein on raised couches, they shall find therein neither (the light of) the sun, nor intense cold. ۝ And close upon them (shall be) its shadows, and its fruits shall be made near (to them), being easy to reach. ۝ And there shall be made to go around them, vessels of silver and goblets which are of glass, ۝ (Transparent as) glass, made of silver; they have measured them according to a measure. ۝ And they shall be made to drink therein a cup the admixture of which will be ginger, ۝ (Of) a fountain therein which is named *Salsabīl*. ۝ And around them will go youths never altering in age; when you see them you will think them to be scattered pearls. ۝ And when you see them, you will see blessings and a great kingdom. ۝ Upon them will be garments of fine green silk and thick silk interwoven with gold, and they shall be adorned with bracelets of silver, and their Lord will make them drink a pure drink. ۝ Surely, this is a reward for you, and your striving will be recompensed."

Great Rewards of Paradise

After a general overview in the previous verses about the salvation granted to the righteous doers from a painful punishment on the Day of Judgement, their reaching to the station of meeting their Beloved and being drowned in pleasure and happiness, the verses currently under review offer an exegesis of the blessings of Paradise. In these verses, a minimum of fifteen bounties have been mentioned.

The first thing spoken about is a place of residence and clothing for the people of Paradise: ﴾And reward them, because they were patient, with garden and silk﴿.

Therefore, in return for the fortitude and self-sacrifice shown in this world, which in one way was displayed by being truthful to their promise made (to Allah ﷻ), by keeping their fasts and donating their food to the poor, orphan, and war captive when the time for breaking the fast came, Allah ﷻ will grant them a special place in the gardens of Paradise and dress them with the best clothing.

It is not only in this verse, but rather other verses of the Quran also clearly show this truth that the rewards on the Day of Resurrection will be given to that person who showed patience and fortitude (patience in the way of obedience, refraining from committing sins, and forbearance in bearing trials and tribulations). In verse 24 of Sūrah al-Raʿd (13), we read that the angels will say the following words to the people of Paradise:

﴿ سَلَامٌ عَلَيْكُمْ بِمَا صَبَرْتُمْ ﴾

> "Peace be upon all of you due for the patience which you endured."

In verse 111 of Sūrah al-Mu'minūn (23), it is mentioned that:

﴿ إِنِّي جَزَيْتُهُمُ الْيَوْمَ بِمَا صَبَرُوا أَنَّهُمْ هُمُ الْفَائِزُونَ ﴾

> "Surely, I will reward those people on that Day (the Day of Judgement) due to the patience which they had; indeed, those people will be the victorious ones."

❁ ❁ ❁

We then read: ﴾Reclining therein on raised couches, they shall find therein neither (the severe heat of) the sun, nor intense cold﴿.

By mentioning their physical state of reclining on raised couches, this points to the comfort and ease which they will experience - for this is how people can usually be seen in this world when they are relaxing.

This verse also points to the perfect weather conditions that will exist in Paradise. It does not tell us that there will be no sun or moon in Paradise, rather, it tells us that if there is a sun, then its rays will not be such so as to trouble people. At the same time, the trees will also cast a shadow which will be used as a shade!

The word *'zamharīr'* comes from the word *'zamhar'* which means 'intense heat,' 'severe anger,' or 'eyes turning red due to the anger a person is feeling,' however in this verse, the first meaning is the correct one. It is further interesting to note that it has been mentioned in the traditions that there is a spot in the Hellfire that is so cold that the body parts will shatter due to it![49]

The original meaning of the word *'arā'ik'* - whose plural is *'arīka'* - are 'tables' or 'platforms' which are found in a bridal room; and in this verse, its meaning is the beautifully decorated, raised platforms which the inhabitants of Paradise will rest upon. The famous commentator of the Ahl al-Sunnah, al-Ālūsī, in his *tafsīr*, *Rūḥ al-Ma'ānī* narrates a tradition from Ibn 'Abbās that:

بَيْنَا أَهْلَ الْجَنَّةِ فِي الْجَنَّةِ إِذَا رَأَوْا ضَوْءًا كَضَوْءِ الشَّمْسِ، وَقَدْ أَشْرَقَتِ الْجِنَانُ بِهِ فَيَقُولُ أَهْلُ الْجَنَّةِ يَا رِضْوَانَ مَا هٰذَا؟ وَقَدْ قَالَ رَبُّنَا لَا يَرَوْنَ

[49] *Tafsīr Durr al-Manthūr*, Vol. 6, Pg. 300.

فِيهَا شَمْسًا وَلاَ زَمْهَرِيرًا، فَيَقُولُ لَهُمْ رِضْوَانٌ لَيْسَ هٰذَا بِشَمْسٍ، وَلاَ قَمَرٍ، وَلٰكِنْ عَلِيٌّ وَفَاطِمَةُ ضَحِكَا، وَأَشْرَقَتِ الْجِنَانُ مِنْ نُورِ ثَغْرَيهِمَا.

"When the people of Paradise are in Paradise, suddenly they will see a light which will resemble the light of the sun through which Paradise will be illuminated. The people of Paradise will ask: 'O Riḍwān (the guardian angel of Heaven), what is this illumination that we are seeing? Our Lord had clearly stated (in the Quran) that: ﴾...they shall find therein neither the light of the sun, nor intense cold﴿?' Riḍwān will reply to them: 'This is not the illumination of the sun, nor the moon, rather, it is 'Alī and Fāṭima laughing, and thus all of Paradise is being illuminated through the light of their teeth!'"[50]

۞ ۞ ۞

The next verse continues with the blessings: ﴾And close upon them (shall be) its shadows and its fruits shall be made near (to them), being easy to reach﴿.[51]

There will be no difficulties in reaching the food, nor will their hands become dirty; they will not even need to expend any energy or move from their seats to get the fruits they want!

Once again, it is important to remind ourselves that the rules which govern human life in this world are drastically different from the next world, and whatever we read about the bounties of Paradise in these and other verses of the Quran are only cursory glances at the expressive bounties which will be present there.

---

[50] *Tafsīr Rūḥ al-Ma'ānī*, Vol. 29, Pg. 159.

[51] The word *'quṭūf'* is the plural of *'qiṭf'* or *'qaṭf'* with a '*kasrah*' or a '*fatha*' on the first letter. The meaning of the first form is the actual trait, while the second word has the infinitive meaning of the word - thus, either a fruit which has been picked from a tree, or to pick some fruit from a tree.

According to some clear traditions that have been mentioned in these regards, there are bounties stored in Paradise which not a single eye has seen yet, not a single ear has heard about; and there are things which no one has ever even thought about!

Ibn ʿAbbās stated the following regarding some of the verses of this chapter: "That which Allah has mentioned in the Quran regarding the pleasures of Paradise have no comparison or example in this material world. However, Allah has referred to these bounties by using names of things which we know and recognize in this world. For example, regarding the pure drink, He calls it *'zanjabīl'* or a drink of ginger since this is an aromatic substance which the ʿArabs have a strong affinity towards."[52]

۞ ۞ ۞

We are then given a glimpse of how the guests of Allah ﷻ will be welcomed into Paradise, what will be at their disposal, and who will serve them: ﴾And there shall be made to go around them vessels of silver, and goblets which are made of glass﴿.

۞ ۞ ۞

The chapter continues: ﴾(Transparent as) glass, made of silver; they have measured them according to a measure﴿.

Containers will hold distinct types of foods in Paradise, and there will also be a variety of refreshing and revitalizing drinks in the silver goblets. People will be able to have as much as they want to eat and drink, and the servants of Paradise will constantly be nearby - ready to always serve them.

The word *'āniyah'* whose plural is *'inā''* refers to any type of dish which food is put into; while the word *'akwāb'* whose plural

---

52 *Tafsīr Majmaʿ al-Bayān*, Vol. 10, Pg. 411.

is *'kūb'* refers to a glass which does not have a handle - sometimes referred to as a tumbler or goblet.

The word *'qawārīr'* whose plural is *'qārūrah'* refers to a crystalline glass; however, the overwhelming point in this verse is that we are told the glasses are "crystalline glasses (see-through), but they are made of silver!" In the world we live in, no such tumbler exists, since crystalline glass cups are made from a special substance which is smelted. However, Allah ﷻ, the One who created particles such as sand and other types of rocks which can then be transformed into transparent, see-through glass by His creations is able to create transparent tumblers made of silver!

From these words, we can deduce that the dishes and tumblers of Paradise will be clear and lucid like glass, however, they will have the brightness, luminance, and beauty of silver, and the drinks which will fill these vessels will be something completely different than what is present in this world!

In a narration from Imām Jaʿfar al-Ṣādiq ؑ, it is mentioned:

يَنْفُذُ الْبَصَرُ فِي فِضَّةِ الْجَنَّةِ كَمَا يَنْفُذُ فِي الْزُجَاجِ.

"In Paradise, a person's eyes will penetrate through silver just like a person's eyes can see through tumblers made of crystal in this transient world."[53]

Also, in our day and age, scientists have been able to discover various types of rays - such as x-rays - which can penetrate through a body and see through it just like a person sees through glass.

Ibn ʿAbbās has stated that: "All of the blessings of Paradise have a comparison and similitude in this world except for the see-through glasses which are made of silver, as there is no comparison to that in this world!"[54]

---

[53] *Tafsīr Majmaʿ al-Bayān*, Vol. 10, Pg. 410.
[54] *Tafsīr Rūḥ al-Maʿānī*, Vol. 29, Pg. 159.

✡✡✡

After this, we read: ﴾And they will be made to drink therein a cup, the fusion of which will be of ginger﴿.

Many exegetes have stated that the pre-Islamic ʿArabs had a passion for a specific type of drink made with ginger, and it had a strong taste to it, and it is for this reason that such a drink has been mentioned in the Quran and will be given to the people of Paradise. However, the difference between these two drinks - the one in this world and that given to the people in Paradise - will be the difference of the earth to the sky! Rather, we can state that the dissimilarity is like the difference between this world and the next one!

From what we understand of the history, the ʿArabs used to enjoy two types of drinks - one brought about joy and happiness, while the other calmed them down and put them into a mellow mood. The first drink was mixed with ginger, while the second one was mixed with camphor. Since the realities of the other world cannot be described and contained in the words we use in this world; we have no choice but to present these concepts with a broad description, and to state that they are greater than the understanding of whatever we have in this world. Various commentaries have been given regarding the ginger spoken about in this section, however, most of the interpretations of this word revolve around an aromatic item used in food and drink.

✡✡✡

We then read: ﴾(Of) a fountain therein which is named *Salsabīl*﴿.[55]

---

[55] Regarding the state of the word *"ʿayna,"* it follows the same pattern and the same word a few verses previous in which *"ʿayna"* was also mentioned. It has been accepted that it is in the accusative state with a type of removal present.

Salsabīl is the word used for this very tasty drink which is easy to consume and is nourishing. Most exegetes of the Quran believe that this word comes from the root *'salāsah'* which means 'something that flows' - just as a person's smooth and flowing words are referred to as being *'salīs.'* Other scholars believe that it comes from the root *'tasalsul'* which means a 'continuous movement.' Thus, in this verse, the meaning could be something like a continuously flowing spring.

Other scholars believe that this word has been constructed from two separate words *'sa-a-la'* and *'sabīl;'* while some consider it as coming from the words *'sāla'* and *'sabīl.'* If we accept this first opinion, then the meaning is 'a path to request something;' while if we take the second opinion, then the meaning is 'they chose a path;' however, the meaning of both is again something which is nourishing.

Various scholars have clearly stated that in the ʿArabic language, the word *'salsabīl'* did not exist, and that the first time it was used was in the Noble Quran.[56] However, the first opinion stated is the most accepted and appropriate understanding.

✪ ✪ ✪

We are then given a description of those who have been invited to this joyous gathering in the presence of the Almighty in Paradise: ﴾And youths, ever altering in age, shall go around them; when you see them you will think them to be scattered pearls﴿.

---

[56] Some exegetists of the Quran state that the word *'salsabīl'* is indeclinable (the last vowel point can never change whatever their grammatical position is) according to the rules of ʿArabic language since it is both a specific noun and a non-ʿArabic word, thus, it has taken its own double-diacritics for it to fit in the same pattern as the end of the other verses in this Sūrah.

Not only will people be in the everlasting Heaven, but even their age, beauty, and youthful state of enjoyment will also remain with them for eternity! In addition, those who will lead them into Paradise will have these same traits, and this can be seen from the words 'for eternity,' and the phrase 'they will encircle them.'

The use of the phrase 'as scattered pearls' is a reference to the beauty, clarity, illumination, and attraction of these individuals - the servants of those in Paradise - and their broad presence in that Divine and spiritual banquet.

۞ ۞ ۞

Seeing as how the blessings of the next life cannot be described - even by using the most expressive and meaningful words in the English language, in the next verse we read: ﴾And when you see them, you shall see blessings and a great kingdom﴿![57]

Various commentaries have been offered for the words 'blessings' and 'a great kingdom.'

There is a tradition from Imām Jaʿfar al-Ṣādiq ﷺ in which he said that the meaning of this verse is the kingdom which will never go away or be destroyed.[58] It may also refer to the blessings of Paradise which will be so numerous that it is not even possible to enumerate them.

The phrase 'a great kingdom' may refer to the angels who will ask the people of Heaven for permission when they want to enter

---

[57] Some exegetes of the Quran have clearly stated that the particle *'thamma'* found in this verse is the adverb of the place, while the word *'ra'ayta'* is in the meaning of the intransitive verb, and thus the meaning of this verse would be: "When you see with your eyes, you will see the blessings and a great kingdom." Another possibility has also been mentioned which states that the *'thamma'* in this verse is the demonstrative pronoun for something far away, and is the object for the transitive verb *'ra'ayta.'*

[58] *Tafsīr Majmaʿ al-Bayān*, Vol. 10, Pg. 411.

the sacred grounds, and upon entering they will greet them with the words of peace; or it may refer to the belief that the people in Paradise will have any wish or desire granted to them. Another meaning of this phrase is in reference to the people in the lowest spiritual rank of Paradise whose jurisdiction of governance will be equivalent to the time it takes to travel 1,000 years in any direction in Paradise; and the final meaning of this phrase is the perpetual and everlasting kingdom which contains all a person's needs and desires.

According to the books of ʿArabic lexicography, the word *'naʿīm'* refers to the 'countless blessings;' while *'mulk kabīr'* refers to the 'greatness and vastness of the gardens in Paradise.' This word covers a broad definition and can include everything mentioned above.

۞ ۞ ۞

Up to now, some of the blessings of Paradise that have been mentioned include houses, couches, shadow of coolness, fruits, drinks, vessels, and groups of servants. At this point, we turn our attention to the objects of beautification which the people of Paradise will be granted: ﴾Upon them will be garments of fine green silk and thick silk interwoven with gold...﴿.

The meaning of *'sundus'* is a 'very thin silk cloth;' while *'istabraq'* refers to a 'thick silk cloth.' Some scholars have stated that the second word has come from the Persian word *'istabar'* or *'stabar'*; while others state that it comes from the ʿArabic word *'barq'* which means 'light' or 'lightning.'

The verse continues and we read: ﴾...and they shall be adorned with bracelets of silver...﴿.

These bracelets of silver are transparent - just like glass - however, they will be more beautiful than rubies and pearls!

The word *'asāwir'* whose plural is *'aswirah,'* which can also be *'sawār'* or *'siwār'* was originally the Persian word *'dastwār'* and means a bracelet, however, when it was imported into the ʿArabic language, its spelling went through a minor change and became *'siwār.'*

The choice of the colour green for the clothing of Paradise is because this colour brings delight and pleasure, just like we see the beautiful leaves on trees. Of course, green also has various tints and hues to it and each of them carries its own special sophistication.

In some verses of the Quran, such as verse 31 of Sūrah al-Kahf (18), we are told that the people of Paradise will be beautified with bracelets of gold:

﴿أُوْلَٰٓئِكَ لَهُمْ جَنَّٰتُ عَدْنٍ تَجْرِي مِن تَحْتِهِمُ ٱلْأَنْهَٰرُ يُحَلَّوْنَ فِيهَا مِنْ أَسَاوِرَ مِن ذَهَبٍ وَيَلْبَسُونَ ثِيَابًا خُضْرًا مِّن سُندُسٍ وَإِسْتَبْرَقٍ مُّتَّكِـِٔينَ فِيهَا عَلَى ٱلْأَرَآئِكِ ۚ نِعْمَ ٱلثَّوَابُ وَحَسُنَتْ مُرْتَفَقًا ﴿٣١﴾﴾

> "These it is for whom are gardens of perpetuity beneath which rivers flow, ornaments shall be given to them therein of bracelets of gold, and they shall wear green robes of fine silk and thick silk brocade interwoven with gold, reclining therein on raised couches; excellent the recompense and goodly the resting place."

This does not conflict with what has been mentioned in the verse under review because it is very well possible that sometimes one will be beautified with bracelets of gold, while at other times another type of bracelet will be worn as mentioned in the verse under review.

At this point a question may arise: Are gold and silver bracelets not only ornaments of beautification for women alone? How is it possible that the men in Paradise will use these forms of adornment?

The answer to this question is clear: In many parts of the world, gold and silver are used as items of beautification for people - even though Islam prohibits men from wearing gold. Of course, there is a difference in the style of the bracelets which people wear, however from verse 53 of Sūrah al-Zukhruf (43) quoting the words of the Pharaoh:

﴿فَلَوْلَا أُلْقِيَ عَلَيْهِ أَسْوِرَةٌ مِّن ذَهَبٍ﴾

> "Why has he (Prophet Mūsā ﷺ) not been given bracelets of gold?"

we see that the wearing of gold bracelets was something that indicated a person's greatness in Egypt at that time. In addition, as we have alluded to many times that when describing the gifts of Paradise, the words used in this world are never sufficient, however there is no other option except to refer to the great pleasures and indescribable blessings of that world with these limited words.

At the end of this verse, in describing the final and most important blessing in this chain of bounties, we read: ﴿...and their Lord will make them drink a pure drink﴾.

In the beginning of this discussion, there was mention about the refreshing drinks which will flow into peoples' cups from the spring of *Salsabīl* that will quench the thirst of the inhabitants of Paradise. However, there is a vast difference between what was previously mentioned and what is stated in this verse!

From one angle, the ones who will quench the thirst are the 'ever-young servants;' and in this verse, the One who will quench the thirst of those in Paradise is Allah ﷻ - and what amazing wording has been used here! Keep in mind that the word used in this verse is *'Rabb'* - a word which tells us that He is the same Creator Who continuously nurtures humanity and is our Ruler and Teacher, and that He has been with us during our entire course of struggling to reach perfection, and when we finally reach that ultimate stage, then we will see His Lordship as it manifests to the highest pinnacles and with the hand of His Power, He will satiate the thirst of His righteous and well-acting servants with a pure drink!

In addition, the word *'ṭahūr'* which is used in this verse refers to something that is 'pure' and has the 'ability to purify' other things. Therefore, this drink will clean the body and spirit of a person from all forms of filth that may be remaining, and will bring about such a sense of spirituality, light, and pleasure with it that it cannot even be described with words!

Imām Jaʿfar al-Ṣādiq ﵇ states:

يُطَهِّرُ هُمْ عَنْ كُلِّ شَيْءٍ سِوىٰ اللّٰهِ.

"(This drink) will purify the heart of a person from everything (within it) except for Allah."[59]

The curtains of negligence will be removed; the spiritual veils will all be shattered; and the believer will be made worthy of remaining eternally in the proximity of Allah ﷻ - an exhilaration which this pure drink will give, and which is greater than any other blessing, and loftier than any other possible gift!

The impure, forbidden drinks of this world corrupt the intellect of people, and spiritually distance them from Allah ﷻ; however, the pure drink which is given by the hands of the Lord in Paradise will make a person negligent of everything other than Him ﷻ - and such a person will become drowned in His Beauty and Majesty! In summary, the subtle points in this verse and all that which is contained in this blessing is greater than any other gift!

In a tradition from the Messenger of Allah ﷺ, we can deduce that the source of this pure drink will be from Paradise itself:

فَيُسْقَوْنَ مِنْهَا شَرْبَةً فَيُطَهِّرُ اللّٰهُ بِهَا قُلُوبُهُمْ مِنَ الْحَسَدِ ... وَذٰلِكَ قَوْلِ اللّٰهِ عَزَّوَجَلَّ ﴿وَسَقَاهُمْ رَبُّهُمْ شَرَابًا طَهُورًا﴾

[59] *Tafsīr Majmaʿ al-Bayān*, Vol. 10, Pg. 411.

> “So then, Allah will give them a drink through which their hearts will become purified from jealousy ... and this is the meaning of the Words of Allah, the Noble and Grand ﴾And their Lord will give them a pure drink﴿.”[60]

It is interesting to note that the word ‘pure’ has been mentioned in the Noble Quran on **only two** occasions - once in Sūrah al-Furqān (25), verse 48 regarding rain which purifies all things and brings the dead back to life; and then again in this verse referring to the pure drink of Paradise which will purify and give a new life:

﴿وَهُوَ ٱلَّذِيٓ أَرۡسَلَ ٱلرِّيَٰحَ بُشۡرَۢا بَيۡنَ يَدَيۡ رَحۡمَتِهِۦۚ وَأَنزَلۡنَا مِنَ ٱلسَّمَآءِ مَآءٗ طَهُورٗا ٤٨﴾

> “And He it is Who sends forth the (merciful) winds as glad tidings in advance of His mercy. And We cause pure water to descend from the sky.”

In the final verse under review in this section, we read: ﴾Surely this is a reward for you, and your striving will be recompensed﴿.

This has been stated in case some people think that these gifts and grand rewards are given for no reason! Rather, these are the rewards for a person’s struggles and righteous actions, self-building, and keeping away from sins.[61] The mere act of mentioning this final statement brings forth unusual spiritual pleasures and a special sense of beauty to it that Allah, the Great, [or His angels] are speaking directly to the righteous and good

---

[60] *Tafsīr Nūr al-Thaqalayn*, Vol. 5, Pg. 485, Ḥadīth no. 60.

[61] There is a sentence which should be taken as being intended here, but not expressly mentioned which reads: ‘It was said to them’ or ‘Allah will say to them.’

doers, and are acknowledging and appreciating them by saying that: "Everything which you are being given is due to your actions, and the struggles which you went through in life are definitely appreciated."

According to some exegetes of the Quran, when it comes to all these blessings and gifts, the greatest one is when Allah ﷻ will thank a person for their righteous deeds!

The use of the past-tense verb *'kāna'* tells us about an action which occurred in the past, and it is possible that this verb has been used as an allusion to the fact that the blessings in Paradise are already prepared for the believers before they arrive there. As an example, when a person wants to invite some important guests to their house, they will make sure that all the necessary arrangements are done before they come to their house.

Section Four - Verses 23 to 26

﴿إِنَّا نَحۡنُ نَزَّلۡنَا عَلَيۡكَ ٱلۡقُرۡءَانَ تَنزِيلٗا ٢٣ فَٱصۡبِرۡ لِحُكۡمِ رَبِّكَ وَلَا تُطِعۡ مِنۡهُمۡ ءَاثِمًا أَوۡ كَفُورٗا ٢٤ وَٱذۡكُرِ ٱسۡمَ رَبِّكَ بُكۡرَةٗ وَأَصِيلٗا ٢٥ وَمِنَ ٱلَّيۡلِ فَٱسۡجُدۡ لَهُۥ وَسَبِّحۡهُ لَيۡلٗا طَوِيلًا ٢٦﴾

"Surely, We Ourselves have sent down the Quran to you revealing (it) in portions. ۞ Therefore, wait patiently for the command of your Lord, and obey not from among them a sinner or an ungrateful one. ۞ And glorify the Name of your Lord in the morning and the evening. ۞ And during a part of the night prostrate to Him and give glory to Him (a) long (part of the) night."

Five Points for Success

From the beginning of this chapter until here, the verses focused on the creation of humanity, followed by everyone's resurrection, and then the Day of Judgement.

The verses in this section present us with words spoken directly to the Prophet ﷺ and contain definite commandments regarding the guidance of humanity and the patience and fortitude which they must display while on this path of life. These verses direct the course which guide us to the astounding bounties and blessings - holding firm to the Quran, following the leadership of the Prophet of Islam ﷺ, and taking inspiration from the commandments which the Prophet ﷺ has been given.

We first read: ﴾Surely, We Ourselves have sent down the Quran to you revealing (it) in portions﴿.

Some exegetes of the Quran have stated that the word 'in portions' used in this verse has been mentioned as an unconditional object and refers to the gradual revelation of the Quran and its effect on the spiritual training of a person. Others have stated that it refers to the greatness and status of the heavenly Book and highlights the fact that the Quran has been revealed by Allah ﷻ - keeping in mind that other forms of emphasis also exist in this verse such as 'surely,' 'We,' and the 'verbal sentence structure' which also acts as a form of emphasis.

Indeed, this verse provides an answer to those who claimed that the Prophet ﷺ was a sooth-sayer, a magician, or was fabricating lies against Allah ﷻ!

۞ ۞ ۞

Five important commandments are then given to the Prophet of Islam ﷺ, the first one being an invitation to patience and fortitude: ﴾Therefore, wait patiently for the command of your Lord...﴿.

The Prophet ﷺ is commanded to disregard any difficulties, obstacles, and the many enemies and opponents on the path of conveying the faith of Islam, and to continue to press forward just as he did in the past. It is interesting to note that the commandment to have fortitude has been mentioned with a *'fā''* which means 'the result' as seen in the word *'faṣbir.'* This means that the revelation of the Quran is from Allah ﷻ, and since Allah ﷻ is the Prophet's assistant and support, then without doubt he ﷺ must have fortitude, and the use of the word 'Lord' is also a subtle allusion to this issue.

The second commandment given to Prophet Muḥammad ﷺ is that he must not compromise with the misguided people: ﴾...and obey not from among them a sinner or an ungrateful one﴿.

This second order highlights the first commandment of being patient which was given to the Prophet ﷺ.

As we know, some of the enemies of Prophet Muḥammad ﷺ tried to divert him to the wrong path using various tactics. It has been mentioned in the narrations that 'Utbah ibn Rabī'ah and Walīd ibn Mughīrah asked the Prophet ﷺ to give up his mission of inviting people towards Islam, and if he complied, then they would give him such a large amount of wealth that he would be taken care of forever. They also promised him the most beautiful ʿArab women as his wives, and many other material bounties!

In the verse under review, Allah ﷻ ordered the Prophet ﷺ, who was a great and truthful leader, to exhibit patience in the face of such satanic whisperings from the people which they will put forth later, and that he must have fortitude in the face of their temptations which will make him a great leader within society! In summary, he was not to submit to them, and not even pay any attention to their threats!

It is true that the Prophet of Islam ﷺ never submitted to such demands, so this verse was simply emphasizing the importance of this subject, and it is also an everlasting lesson for all leaders who are treading the path of Allah ﷻ.

Although some exegetes of the Quran have stated that the word 'sinner' refers to ʿUtbah ibn Rabīʿah, and 'ingrate disbeliever' refers to Walīd ibn Mughīrah or Abū Jahl - and all three of them were from the polytheistic ʿArabs, however it is clear that both 'sinner' and 'ungrateful disbeliever' and 'one who makes others disbelieve' are words with broad applications and can refer to all sinners and polytheists - even if the three individuals noted were the most obvious examples of these traits.

It should also be noted that the word 'sinner' has a general understanding to it which includes those who are referred to as an 'ingrate disbeliever.' Therefore, mentioning the word 'ingrate disbeliever' is referred to in the ʿArabic language as 'mentioning a specific term after a general term' and is done to accentuate the discussion.

Since patience and perseverance in the face of the tirade of enormous challenges is not something easy, and traversing this path requires two abilities, we then read: ﴾And glorify the Name of your Lord in the morning and the evening﴿.

❂ ❂ ❂

We are then told: ﴾And during a part of the night, prostrate to Him, and give glory to Him (a) long (part of the) night﴿.

This act of praying during the night should be done so that under the shade of the remembrance *(dhikr)*, prostration *(sajdah)*, and glorification *(tasbīḥ)*, the required power and spiritual strength and assistance needed to struggle against the difficulties of this path can be harnessed.

In this verse, the word *'bukrah'* refers to the beginning of the day, while the word *'aṣīl'* refers to the end of the day or the evening time. Some scholars have stated that the word *'aṣīl'* which refers to the end of the day comes from the root word *'aṣl,'* and this is because the end of the day makes up the initial or earliest part of the night. From other phrases used, we can deduce that the word *'aṣīl'* is sometimes used in reference to the time gap between mid-day and sunset, as can be seen in *Al-Mufradāt* of Rāghib. From the opinions of other scholars, we understand that the word *'aṣīl'* refers to the beginning of the night, and they explain this word as meaning the same as *"ishā'* because this word refers to the commencement of the night - just as the *Ṣalāt* of *Maghrib* and *'Ishā* can be referred to as *'Ishā'ayn* (lit. the two *'Ishā* prayers). In addition, we deduce from the opinion of other scholars that *"ishā'* includes the time from the decline of the sun at noon until the morning of the next day.

However, keeping in mind that the word *'aṣīl'* which has been mentioned in this verse as the opposite of 'morning,' plus we read a discussion regarding worship in the night, the meaning of this word in the verse is the last part of the day just before the night period.

In any case, these two verses illustrate the necessity of paying constant attention to the Pure Essence of Allah ﷻ - both night and day.

Some scholars have stated that this verse is a specific reference to the five daily prayers *(Ṣalawāt)* of *Fajr*, *Ẓuhr*, *ʿAṣr*, *Maghrib*, and *ʿIshā*; or it is in relation to *Ṣalāt al-Layl*. However, the apparent reading is that these prayers *(Ṣalawāt)* are the clearest proofs of this continuous remembrance of Allah ﷻ and the glorification and prostration to Him.

The phrase 'a long portion of the night' is in reference to a significant part of the night which must be kept aside for the glorification of Allah ﷻ; and when Imām ʿAlī al-Riḍā ؑ was asked about this verse and what the meaning of the glorification *(tasbīḥ)* was, he replied: "This refers to *Ṣalāt al-Layl* (the Night Prayer)."[62]

However, it is not unlikely to assume that the exegesis he offered is only the clearest understanding of this verse, and there may be other commentaries possible since *Ṣalāt al-Layl* plays a very important role in strengthening the spirit of true faith, purification of the soul, and keeping alive a person's intention of obeying the commandments of Allah ﷻ.

✧ ✧ ✧

At this point, we must take notice that although the commandments given in the above verses made up a part of the regiment of the Prophet of Islam ﷺ, however in reality, these verses contain lessons for all people who are traversing the path of spiritual and societal leadership and are working for the guidance of humanity.

Therefore, we must know that after gaining complete certainty, possessing perfect faith, and receiving the message which one must convey, it is necessary to observe patience and perseverance,

---

[62] *Tafsīr Majmaʿ al-Bayān*, Vol. 10, Pg. 413.

and not have any fear while facing difficulties on this path, since guiding people - especially when a person is put face to face with those who are unaware of the truth, and in which the strong-headed enemies are present - is something which is always fret with great difficulties. Thus, if a person is not led by patience and fortitude, then no message will ever be triumphant!

At the next stage, a person must struggle and forge ahead with full energy and resilience in the face of the whisperings of the Satanic forces - which include the open sinners and disbelievers - and whatever evil plans and plots they may use to misguide the leaders of society and try to erase the life-giving messages from humanity. Such leaders must not be fooled by the wicked plans or whisperings of anyone, nor can they permit the threats that such people give to the spiritual leaders to find a way into their psyche.

Therefore, to achieve spiritual power in all stages, gain a firm determination, acquire deeply rooted resolve, and an iron-clad decision-making process, a leader must be in the remembrance of Allah ﷻ at every moment - morning and evening! They must prostrate and humble themselves in His presence - especially in the Night Prayers and vigils - and through these prayers and supplications, ask Him for help. If this is conducted, then success will be guaranteed. If a person is faced with tribulations or defeat in any of these stages, then through the benefit of the principles mentioned in these verses quoted and the five acts mentioned, a person will be able to make up one's spiritual losses. Thus, those who are travelling this path should take the course of spiritual building from the Prophet of Islam ﷺ, and his invitation and message, and follow these things in one's own life to attain success!

Section Five - Verses 27 to 31

﴿إِنَّ هَٰٓؤُلَآءِ يُحِبُّونَ ٱلْعَاجِلَةَ وَيَذَرُونَ وَرَآءَهُمْ يَوْمًا ثَقِيلًا ﴿٢٧﴾ نَّحْنُ خَلَقْنَٰهُمْ
وَشَدَدْنَآ أَسْرَهُمْ ۖ وَإِذَا شِئْنَا بَدَّلْنَآ أَمْثَٰلَهُمْ تَبْدِيلًا ﴿٢٨﴾ إِنَّ هَٰذِهِۦ تَذْكِرَةٌ ۖ فَمَن
شَآءَ ٱتَّخَذَ إِلَىٰ رَبِّهِۦ سَبِيلًا ﴿٢٩﴾ وَمَا تَشَآءُونَ إِلَّآ أَن يَشَآءَ ٱللَّهُ ۚ إِنَّ ٱللَّهَ كَانَ
عَلِيمًا حَكِيمًا ﴿٣٠﴾ يُدْخِلُ مَن يَشَآءُ فِى رَحْمَتِهِۦ ۚ وَٱلظَّٰلِمِينَ أَعَدَّ لَهُمْ عَذَابًا
أَلِيمًا ﴿٣١﴾﴾

"Surely, these people love the transitory world, and neglect a grievous Day before them. ۞ We created them and made firm their make, and when We please, We will bring in their place the likes of them by a change. ۞ Surely, this is a reminder, so whoever wishes may take a way to one's Lord. ۞ And you do not will except that which Allah Wills, surely Allah is All-Knowing, All-Wise. ۞ He makes whom He pleases to enter His Mercy; and (as for) the unjust, He has prepared for them a painful chastisement."

This is a Warning Call

In the previous verses, the Prophet ﷺ was warned that he must never fall under the influence of two groups of people - the 'sinners' and the 'disbelievers.' According to history, these two designations were manifest by people who thought they could influence the determination and objective of the Prophet ﷺ, and that they could bribe him with wealth, status, and beautiful women; and these verses under review offer us a greater description of those people.

We first read: ﴾Surely, these people love the transitory world, and neglect a grievous Day which is before them﴿.

The views of such people do not go past spiritual negligence and the fulfillment of the lower desires, and their only sphere of reason is regarding attaining uninhibited, material pleasures. It is astonishing to see that such people wanted the Noble Prophet ﷺ to be just like they were! However, these naive and spiritually blinded individuals decided to ignore the momentous days which await them - tragic days from the point of view of the punishment therein, the accountability for the deeds they performed, the length of time these days will last, and the disgrace and dishonour that these people will face.

The use of the phrase 'behind them' should technically speaking, be another word which conveys the meaning of 'the Day which is in front of them (to come);' however, the phrase 'behind them' has been used because that is a Day which they have entirely forgotten about, and it can be said that they have thrown that Day behind their backs! According to some exegetes of the Quran though, the word *'warā'a'* can sometimes be used in the meaning of behind, and other times for something which is in front of a person.[63]

These people are then warned that they should not feel proud about their power because this is something which Allah ﷻ has granted to them, and anytime He wants, He can instantly take these things away from them.

In this verse, we read: ❮We created them and made firm their make, and when We please, We will bring in their place the likes of them by a change❯.[64]

---

[63] In the commentary of the book, *Rūḥ al-Bayān*, Vol. 8, Pg. 439, it has been mentioned that if *'warā'a'* is annexed to a verb, then it carries the meaning of 'behind,' however if it is annexed with an object, then it is in the meaning of 'in front.'

[64] This verse has a sentence which must be taken as being intended by Allah ﷻ, but not expressly mentioned and can be presumed as being:

The primary meaning of the word *'asar'* was 'to tie something up with a chain' and it is for this reason that captives are referred to as *'asīr'* since they are normally tied up with chains. However, in this verse, the word *'asar'* refers to the strong relationships within a person's essence (that bind things together within them) which give them the ability to conduct important tasks. In this verse, the Quran points to an extremely focused aspect of the physical life which is the various relationships that exist in the numerous body parts of a human being, such as nerves of various sizes that connect all the body parts with one another, just like iron joins various parts of a large machine. This connection between body parts includes things such as ligaments and tendons which join with bones of assorted sizes and the flesh of the body. All of this is put together and forms one complete unit which is ready and able to conduct different activities. This verse also points to the power and strength of a person.

In addition to this verse elucidating upon the Self-Sufficiency and Needlessness of anything which are traits of Allah ﷻ alone, it also refers to the fact that He does not even need the obedience or faith of His creations! Through this verse, people are made aware that if there is even a whisper of true faith within them, then, this is a grace and mercy from their Lord! This can be seen in verse 133 of Sūrah al-Anʿām (6) where we read:

﴿وَرَبُّكَ الْغَنِيُّ ذُو الرَّحْمَةِ إِنْ يَشَأْ يُذْهِبْكُمْ وَيَسْتَخْلِفْ مِنْ بَعْدِكُمْ مَا يَشَاءُ...﴾

'بَدَّلْنَاهُمْ أَمْثَالَهُمْ' which means "(We replaced them with their likes)." It must be noted that the verb 'to change' usually takes two objects, thus in this case, the pronoun in *'hum'* is the first object, while *'amthālahum'* is the second object.

"And your Lord is the Self-Sufficient, the Possessor of Mercy. If He wishes, He will remove all of you and bring others to your place whomsoever He wishes..."

The next verse combines all the discussions which have taken place in this chapter up until this point which make up a complete program for happiness in life: ﴾Surely, this is a reminder, so whoever pleases may take a way to one's Lord﴿.

This verse tells us that: "It is Allah's responsibility to show the True Path - however, there is no compulsion to choose this path. It is us ourselves who, with our intellect and reasoning, must distinguish between truth and falsehood, and through our own decision-making process, make the choice." This point merely emphasizes what was mentioned at the beginning of this chapter in the third verse:

﴿إِنَّا هَدَيْنَاهُ السَّبِيلَ إِمَّا شَاكِرًا وَإِمَّا كَفُورًا﴾

"Surely, We have shown them the way: they may be thankful or unthankful."

At this point, it is possible that simple-minded people may take the previous verse as implying that human beings have been given complete free-will to do as they please, however, in the verse which follows, this incorrect notion is rejected: ﴾And you do not will except that which Allah Wills, surely Allah is All-Knowing, All-Wise﴿.[65]

[65] As for what is the inflection or nuance of 'إِنْ يَشَاءَ اللَّهُ'? A group of exegetes of the Quran have stated that it is in a state of the 'accusative or subjunctive case' due to it being the pronoun denoting time, and thus this

This is the case since: ﴾Surely, Allah is All-Knowing, All-Wise﴿.

This proves the well-known belief of 'a command between the two commands.' From one aspect, we are told that: "Now that Allah has shown you the path, the choice is up to you." At the same time, we are told: "Your choice is dependent upon the Will of Allah." This means that we do not have complete free-will. Rather, the power, ability, and freedom to choose is granted to us through the permission of Allah ﷻ and anytime He wishes, He can take away our power of free choice! Thus, there is no 'complete freedom,' nor is there 'complete compulsion' - rather there is a fine and subtle truth between these two states. In other words, there is a form of freedom which is related directly to the Will of Allah ﷻ which can, at any time, be taken away so that the servants can fulfill the responsibility and accountability on their shoulders, and in which lies the secret of how they can reach perfection, and through which they realize that they are not completely needless of Allah ﷻ.

In brief, this verse shows that everyone is a servant of Allah ﷻ and thus one must realize that they are not completely free from need of guidance, help, success, and His assistance; while at the same time, when they decide to do something, they submit themselves to Him and work with His assistance.

From this discussion, when some exegetes of the Quran such as Fakhr al-Dīn al-Rāzī, subscribe to the belief of compulsion in all affairs, they do so by holding onto this verse due to some pre-conceived notions they have regarding this issue. He himself (Fakhr al-Dīn al-Rāzī) has been quoted as saying:

---

phrase would mean 'مَا تَشَاوُنَ إِلَّا وَقْتُ مَشِيَّةِ اللّٰهِ' - 'You will not desire except when the time comes for what Allah decides.' However, another supposition also exists which states that 'شيئا' is in the elliptical, and thus this phrase means 'وَ مَا تَشَاؤُنَ إِلَّا شَيْئًا يَشَآءَ اللّٰهُ' - 'You will not desire anything except that Allah first decides that thing before-hand.'

وَاعْلَمْ أَنَّ هٰذِهِ الْآيَةِ مِنْ جُمْلَةِ الْآيَاتِ الَّتِي تَلَاطَمَتْ فِيهَا أَمْوَاجُ الْجَبْرِ وَالْقَدْرِ.

> “Know that this verse is one of those verses in which the rough waves of compulsion and predestination ride!”[66]

Indeed, if this verse is separated from that which came before it, then this baseless belief could be accepted; however, by keeping in mind that there is a discussion of free-will, while in another verse there is a discussion about the Will of Allah ﷻ, thus this issue of ‘A command between the two affairs’ becomes understandable.

It is remarkable to see the supporters of the belief of free-will also hold on to this verse of the Quran and speak about complete free-will, while those who believe in compulsion in all actions are only able to perceive this belief of theirs - each party wanting to justify their preconceived notions and beliefs using these verses! We see that the correct understanding of the Word of Allah ﷻ and any other speech always necessitates passing of judgement by looking at whatever is spoken as one unit without any prejudice or prejudgements.

The end of this verse tells us that: ﴾Surely, Allah is All-Knowing, All-Wise﴿.

This may refer to the same thing stated above because the Knowledge and Wisdom of Allah ﷻ demand that the servants freely travel the path towards perfection. If this was not the case, then perfection which comes through compulsion and force is not really perfection!

In addition, the Knowledge, and Wisdom of Allah ﷻ does not permit a person to be forced to do good or bad deeds, and then reward the good doers who were forced to do honourable deeds or punish the bad doers who were forced to perform bad deeds.

---

[66] *Tafsīr al-Kabīr*, Vol. 30, Pg. 262.

Finally, in the last verse of this chapter, we see the outcome of the good and bad doers as has been mentioned in one short, yet meaningful sentence: ﴾He makes whom He pleases to enter His Mercy; and (as for) the unjust, He has prepared for them a painful chastisement﴿.

The beginning of this verse tells us that He makes those whom He wishes to enter His Mercy, however, at the end we read that the punishment will surround the oppressors, and this clearly shows us that His prerogative to punish follows humankind's desire to commit oppression and sins!

By taking the opposite of this analogy, it becomes clear that His intention to shower mercy on humanity follows the intention of humanity to bring about true faith, perform righteous actions, and enact justice in their daily lives - and this cannot be expected from anyone except the people who perform their actions with wisdom!

It is interesting to note that even with this clear analogy that has been given, people still exist, such as Fakhr al-Dīn al-Rāzī, who state that the beginning of this verse was proof for the existence of compulsion, without realizing that the end of this verse proves the freedom of intention and actions of the oppressors![67]

---

[67] A detailed discussion on the issue of this verse which deals with the intention can be seen in Vol. 19 of *Tafsīr Nemunah*, Pp. 461-468, and under the commentary of verse 37 of Sūrah al-Zumar.

O Allah! Enter us into Your Mercy, and distance us from the painful punishment which awaits the oppressors!

O Allah! You have shown us the path, and we too have made the intention to follow this path, therefore please help us in this!

O Allah! If we are not among the righteous people, then at least You know that we are among those who love those individuals, so please join us with them in the eventual abode!

So be it, O Lord of all the Worlds.

End of Sūrah al-Insān (Sūrah al-Dahr)

Fāṭima al-Zahrā' عليها السلام in the Noble Quran

Sūrah al-Qadr

The Chapter of the (Night of) Ordainment or Power

This chapter was revealed in Mecca and contains 5 verses

Sūrah al-Qadr

Contents of Sūrah al-Qadr

As can be understood from its name, this chapter refers to the revelation of the Noble Quran on the Night of Ordainment *(Laylatul Qadr)*, and then describes the importance of the night and the blessings within it.

One should ask: Was this chapter revealed in Mecca or Medina? Amongst the commentators, it is widely known as a Meccan chapter; although some hold that it was revealed in Medina because of a narration which states that the Noble Prophet ﷺ dreamt that the *Umayyads* were climbing his pulpit *(mimbar)*. It very much disturbed the Prophet ﷺ to have such a dream, so Sūrah al-Qadr was revealed to comfort him. Therefore, some people believe that the verse: "The Night of *Qadr* is better than a thousand months" refers to the length of time that the *Umayyads* governed, which was about one thousand months. In addition, we know that the Masjid and *mimbar* (pulpit) were established in Medina, not in Mecca.[68]

However, as stated above, this chapter is more well-known as a Meccan one; and the other opinion may be a kind of application not related directly to the occasion of revelation.

Virtues of Studying this Chapter

Regarding the benefits of studying this sūrah , there is a narration from Prophet Muḥammad ﷺ which states:

مَنْ قَرَأَهَا أُعْطِيَ مِنَ الْأَجْرِ كَمَنْ صَامَ رَمَضَانَ وَأَحْيَا لَيْلَةَ الْقَدْرِ.

[68] *Tafsīr Rūḥ al-Ma'ānī*, Vol. 30, Pg. 188; and *Tafsīr Durr al-Manthūr*, Vol. 6, Pg. 391.

> "A person who recites it (Sūrah al-Qadr) will be rewarded like the one who fasted the entire month of Ramaḍān and kept vigil the entire night of *al-Qadr.*"[69]

A narration from Imām Muḥammad al-Bāqir ‎ﷺ says:

مَنْ قَرَأَ ﴿إِنَّا أَنْزَلْنَاهُ﴾ بِجَهْرٍ كَانَ كَشَاهِرِ سَيْفِهِ فِي سَبِيلِ اللّٰهِ وَمَنْ قَرَأَهَا سِرًّا كَانَ كَالْمُتَشَحِّطِ بِدَمِهِ فِي سَبِيلِ اللّٰهِ.

> "A person who recites 'Indeed, We have revealed it (Sūrah al-Qadr)' in an audible voice is like a person who fights in the way of Allah with their sword drawn; and the one who recites it in an audible whisper is like a person who drowns in one's own blood for the sake of Allah (due to being killed in the battlefield)."[70]

It is obvious that such rewards are not for that person who merely recites the chapter and does not comprehend its real meanings; rather, such rewards are reserved for that person who recites this chapter, understands its contents, and then embellishes all of their daily actions with its comprehensive teachings, and considers the Quran as something important and implements its verses in one's daily life.

---

[69] *Tafsīr Majmaʿ al-Bayān*, Vol. 30, Pg. 516.

[70] Ibid.

بِسْمِ اللَّهِ الرَّحْمَٰنِ الرَّحِيمِ

In the Name of Allah, the All-Compassionate, the All-Merciful

Section One - Verses 1 to 5

﴿إِنَّآ أَنزَلۡنَٰهُ فِي لَيۡلَةِ ٱلۡقَدۡرِ ١ وَمَآ أَدۡرَىٰكَ مَا لَيۡلَةُ ٱلۡقَدۡرِ ٢ لَيۡلَةُ ٱلۡقَدۡرِ
خَيۡرٞ مِّنۡ أَلۡفِ شَهۡرٖ ٣ تَنَزَّلُ ٱلۡمَلَٰٓئِكَةُ وَٱلرُّوحُ فِيهَا بِإِذۡنِ رَبِّهِم مِّن كُلِّ أَمۡرٖ
٤ سَلَٰمٌ هِيَ حَتَّىٰ مَطۡلَعِ ٱلۡفَجۡرِ ٥﴾

"Surely, We revealed it (the Quran) on the Night of Ordainment. ۝ And what will make you know what the Night of Ordainment is? ۝ The Night of Ordainment is better than a thousand months. ۝ The angels and the Spirit descend therein by their Lord's permission with every affair. ۝ Peace it is, until the rising of the dawn."

Revelation of the Quran

When we review the verses of the Noble Quran, we can conclude that this Book was revealed in the blessed month of Ramaḍān:

﴿شَهْرُ رَمَضَانَ الَّذِي أُنْزِلَ فِيهِ الْقُرْآنُ...﴾

> "The month of Ramaḍān (is the one) in which the Quran was revealed (sent down)..."[71]

From the apparent reading of this verse, the entire Quran was revealed in the month of Ramaḍān; and in the first verse of Sūrah al-Qadr, we are additionally told:

---

[71] Quran, Sūrah al-Baqarah (2), verse 185.

﴿إِنَّا أَنزَلْنَاهُ فِي لَيْلَةِ الْقَدْرِ﴾

> "Surely, We sent it (the Quran) down on the night of Ordainment *(Laylatul Qadr).*"

Even though in the above-mentioned verse, the word 'Quran' is not explicitly mentioned, however, it is certain that the objective pronoun existing in the phrase 'Surely, We sent **it**' refers to the Quran, and its being mentioned in this format is to show its greatness and importance.

The phrase "Surely, We sent **it**" is another indicator which shows the importance of this great Heavenly-sent Book for which Allah ﷻ has attributed its descent to Himself - and that too by using the plural pronoun 'We' which further shows the Quran's greatness.

The descent of the Quran on the Night of Ordainment, the very night on which the fate of every human being is decided, is another way to show the importance of this Divine Book in its role in forging the destiny of people around the world.

With the combination of the meaning of this verse as just stated, and the above verse from Sūrah al-Baqarah, we can conclude that the Night of Ordainment is in the month of Ramaḍān - however, which night is it? It is not clearly understood from the Quran which night during the month of Ramaḍān the Night of Ordainment is, and indeed this has been left as a mystery for us, however, there are many indicators about it in the narrations which will be dealt with later in the exegesis of this chapter.

Here, a question arises regarding the history and content of the Noble Quran in connection with the events during the life of Prophet Muḥammad ﷺ.

Most clearly, this Heavenly Book was revealed gradually over a period of 23 years, so how does this fit with the above verse which says: ﴾Surely, We sent it (the Quran) down on the Night of Ordainment *(Laylatul Qadr*﴿ during the month of Ramaḍān?

The reply to this question, as many scholars have stated, is to say that the Quran has two kinds of revelation:

1. The first is the revelation of the entire Quran at one time, in one night, to the blessed heart of the Noble Prophet ﷺ; or to *Bayt al-Ma'mūr* - the Frequented House; or from the *Lawḥ al-Maḥfūẓ* - the Preserved Tablet - which is up in the Heavens to the lowest sky of this world.
2. The second kind of revelation is that the Noble Quran came down in portions, gradually, during the entire period of the Prophethood of the final Messenger, which lasted 23 years.[72]

Some commentators have also said that the initiation of the revelation of the Quran began on the Night of Ordainment, but it was not the entire Book which was revealed on that night. However, this idea does not fit with the apparent meaning of the verse which says: ﴾Surely, We sent it (the Quran) down on the Night of Ordainment﴿.

It should be noted that regarding the descent of the Quran, some of the verses have made use of the notion of *'inzāl,'* while other verses speak about *'tanzīl.'* From a review of some Arabic dictionaries, we understand that the difference between these two Arabic terms is that *'inzāl'* has a broad meaning, and here it implies 'bringing down all at once;' while *'tanzīl'* implies 'bringing down gradually.'[73]

This difference, which is seen in various verses of the Quran, can be taken as an indication to the above mentioned two types of descent.

---

[72] A deeper explanation of this division of the method of revelation has been covered under the exegesis of verse 3 of Sūrah al-Dukhān which is in Volume 21 of *Tafsīr Nemunah* on Page 148 and beyond.

[73] *Al-Mufradāt*, under the letters *'na-za-la.'*

In the next verse, referring to the greatness of the Night of Ordainment, it says: ﴾And what will make you know (comprehend) what the Night of Ordainment is﴿?

Right after this, we are told: ﴾The Night of Ordainment is better than a thousand months﴿.

This phrase shows that the importance of this Night is so great that even the Noble Prophet ﷺ, with his vast knowledge, did not know the status of this Night prior to it being revealed to him!

We know that one thousand months is more than eighty years, and truly what a great night it is who's worth and value is as much as the length of a long-blessed life which a person could have.

It is cited in some commentaries that the Noble Prophet ﷺ said: "One of the members of the Children of Isrā'īl spent one thousand months with his fighting armour on and was always prepared for war in the path of Allah." The companions of the Prophet ﷺ became surprised and wished that there might have been that sort of virtue and honour for them as well, and it was at this time that the above verse came down which said: ﴾The Night of Ordainment is better than a thousand months﴿.[74]

In another tradition, the Prophet ﷺ has been quoted as speaking about four individuals from among the Children of Isrā'īl who worshipped Allah for a consecutive span of 80 years each, and during this time committed no acts of transgression against His orders. The companions of the Prophet ﷺ upon hearing this all wished that they too could have been so fortunate, and it was at this time that the above quoted verse was revealed.[75]

---

[74] *Tafsīr Durr al-Manthūr*, Vol. 6, Pg. 371.

[75] *Tafsīr Durr al-Manthūr*, Vol. 6, Pg. 371.

A question comes up that: Is the amount of 'one thousand' which is mentioned in this verse in the meaning of the actual number of 1,000, or does it refer to a 'multitude?' Some scholars say that the figure given of 'one thousand' mentioned in this verse is for augmentation denoting that the value of the Night of Ordainment is more than thousands of months; but the above-mentioned narrations indicate that this figure, which is used shows the actual amount, and generally figures are used to show numbers, except for the time when clear evidence for augmentation is available.

۞۞۞

Then, describing the Night of Ordainment in greater detail, Allah says: ﴾The Angels and the Spirit descend therein by their Lord's permission with every affair﴿.

Regarding the term *'tanazzala'* which is a future tense verb with the sense of continuity and comes from the root *'tatanazzala,'* this word makes it clear that the Night of Ordainment is not only for the time period of the Noble Prophet ﷺ and the era in which the descent of the Quran was taking place, rather it is a permanent fixture in the religion, and it is a Night that will repeat over again every single year until the end of time.

As for the meaning of "*al-Rūḥ* - the Spirit," some commentators state that it refers to Angel Jibrā'īl, the trustworthy one, who is also called *"Rūḥ al-Amīn"* in the Quran. Other scholars have rendered the meaning of *"al-Rūḥ* - the Spirit" to mean 'Divine revelation' and have used verse 52 of Sūrah al-Shūra to prove this:

﴿وَكَذَٰلِكَ أَوْحَيْنَا إِلَيْكَ رُوحًا مِنْ أَمْرِنَا...﴾

"And thus, have We revealed to you the Spirit of Our command (the Quran)...".[76]

In this case, the meaning of the verse would become: "The Angels, along with the Divine revelation, descend therein with every affair."

There is also a third commentary which seems the most appropriate of all which states that *"al-Rūḥ - the Spirit"* is an important creation of Allah which is greater than the angels; just as it has been mentioned in a tradition from Imām Jaʿfar al-Ṣādiq in which a person asked him whether *"al-Rūḥ"* was the same as Angel Jibrāʾīl or not, to which he replied:

جِبْرَائِيلُ مِنَ الْمَلَائِكَةِ وَالرُّوحُ أَعْظَمُ مِنَ الْمَلَائِكَةِ. أَلَيْسَ أَنَّ اللّهَ عَزَّوَجَلَّ يَقُولُ: ﴿تَنَزَّلُ الْمَلَائِكَةُ وَالرُّوحُ؟﴾

"Jibrāʾīl is one of the angels and *al-Rūḥ* (the Spirit) is even greater than the angels. Has Allah, the Exalted, not said: ﴿The angels and the Spirit descend?﴾".[77]

This means that in the sequence of comparison, these two - meaning Jibrāʾīl and *al-Rūḥ* - are different entities.

There are also other commentaries cited on the word *"al-Rūḥ,"* but as they do not have any supporting evidence, we will not mention them here.

The meaning of 'with every affair' is that the angels descend to proportionate and assign the fates, and to bring the blessings and goodness on that Night, and it is the fulfillment of these actions which is the purpose of their descent. In addition, it may be stated that they also bring any good affair and different fates (for all of humanity). Other scholars have opined that the meaning is that

---

[76] Quran, Sūrah al-Shūra (42), verse 52.
[77] *Tafsīr al-Burhān*, Vol. 4, Pg. 481.

they descend by the command of Allah ﷻ, however, the very first meaning is the most befitting.

The meaning of 'their Lord' - of which the emphasis is about Lordship and management of the world - has a close relationship with the action of these angels, saying that they descend to proportionate and assign the affairs, and their accomplishment is a part of the Lordship of Allah ﷻ.

۞۞۞

In the last verse of this chapter, it says: ﴾Peace it is, until the rising of the dawn﴿.

It is a Night on which both the Quran descended, and worship and spiritual vigilance therein is equal to a thousand months; in addition, it is a Night in which Divine Blessings come down, and one in which His special Mercy covers all creatures; lastly, it is also a Night in which the angels and the Spirit descend. Thus, it is a Night full of peace and benedictions - from the beginning to the end - in which, according to some narrations, even Satan is fastened in chains, and from this point of view, this Night is also one of spiritual security.

Therefore, the use of the word *"salām* - peace" which means 'peace and safety' (instead of the word 'safe') has been employed, because a kind of emphasis is also contained in this - just like it is sometimes said that "Such and such a person is the epitome of justice." Thus, Allah is saying that this Night is the "complete manifestation of peace and safety."

Some have also said that using the word 'peace' regarding that Night is because the angels greet one another, or they greet the believers, or that they are present with the Prophet ﷺ and his sinless successors ﷺ and they greet them - and to combine all of these commentaries together is also possible.

In any case, it is a Night filled with Divine light, grace, mercy, blessings, goodness, spiritual safety, and felicity which is unique in all aspects!

It is cited in a tradition that Imām Muḥammad al-Bāqir ﷺ was asked if he knew which night the Night of Ordainment *(Laylatul Qadr)* was, to which he replied:

كَيْفَ لاَ نَعْرِفُ وَالْمَلاَئِكَةُ تَطُوفُ بِنَا فِيهَا؟

> "How can we not know it when the angels go around us therein?"[78]

In the story of Prophet Ibrāhīm ﷺ, we find that a few of the angels of the Divine came to him and greeted him, and gave him the glad tidings of a son:

﴿وَلَقَدْ جَاءَتْ رُسُلُنَا إِبْرَاهِيمَ بِالْبُشْرَى قَالُوا سَلاَمًا قَالَ سَلاَمٌ فَمَا لَبِثَ أَنْ جَآءَ بِعِجْلٍ حَنِيذٍ ۞ فَلَمَّا رَأَى أَيْدِيَهُمْ لاَ تَصِلُ إِلَيْهِ نَكِرَهُمْ وَأَوْجَسَ مِنْهُمْ خِيفَةً قَالُوا لاَ تَخَفْ إِنَّا أُرْسِلْنَا إِلَى قَوْمِ لُوطٍ ۞ وَامْرَأَتُهُ قَائِمَةٌ فَضَحِكَتْ فَبَشَّرْنَاهَا بِإِسْحَاقَ وَمِنْ وَرَاءِ إِسْحَاقَ يَعْقُوبَ ۞ قَالَتْ يَا وَيْلَتَا أَأَلِدُ وَأَنَا عَجُوزٌ وَهٰذَا بَعْلِي شَيْخًا إِنَّ هٰذَا لَشَيْءٌ عَجِيبٌ ۞ قَالُوا أَتَعْجَبِينَ مِنْ أَمْرِ اللهِ رَحْمَةُ اللهِ وَبَرَكَاتُهُ عَلَيْكُمْ أَهْلَ الْبَيْتِ إِنَّهُ حَمِيدٌ مَجِيدٌ﴾

> "And certainly, Our messengers (angels) came to Ibrāhīm with the good news, and they said: 'Peace!' So he replied: 'Peace!' Then he brought [for them] a roasted calf. But when he saw their hands not reaching for it, he took them amiss and felt a fear for them. They said: 'Do not be afraid. We have been sent to the people of Lūṭ (Lot).' His wife, standing

[78] *Tafsīr al-Burhān*, Vol. 4, Pg. 488, Ḥadīth 29.

> by, laughed as We gave her the good news of [the birth of] Isḥāq (Isaac), and after Isḥāq, Yaʿqūb (Jacob). She said: 'Woe to me! Shall I, an old woman, bear [children], [while] this husband of mine is an old man?! Indeed, this is an odd thing!' They said: 'Are you amazed at Allah's decree? [That is] Allah's mercy and His blessings upon you, people of the household. Indeed, He is All-Praiseworthy, All-Glorious.'"[79]

It is said that all that is contained in this world was worthless in comparison with the delight that Ibrāhīm ﷺ took in that greeting of the angels. Now if we consider that the Night of Ordainment is one in which angels come to the believers in groups and greet them - how delightful it would be (for a believer)!

When Ibrāhīm ﷺ was thrown into the fire which Nimrod ordered to be fuelled to persecute him, the angels came and greeted him, and he remained safe. Can the fire of Hell, under the grace of the angel's greeting to the believers on the Night of Ordainment, not become cool and a means of safety for the believers?

This is the sign of the greatness of the nation of Prophet Muḥammad ﷺ that in that first example, the angels descended to Prophet Ibrāhīm ﷺ, but here, the angels descend upon the believers in Islam![80]

What is Determined on that Night?

To answer this question on why this Night is called the Night of *Qadr*, various opinions have been expressed, including the following:

1. It is called the Night of *Qadr* because all the affairs and the destinies of humanity for the following year are

---

[79] Quran, Sūrah al-Hūd (11), verses 69-73.

[80] *Tafsīr al-Kabīr*, Vol. 32, Pg. 36.

determined; and the third, fourth and fifth verses of Sūrah al-Dukhān (chapter 44) serve as witness to this idea, saying:

﴿إِنَّآ أَنزَلۡنَٰهُ فِي لَيۡلَةٖ مُّبَٰرَكَةٍۚ إِنَّا كُنَّا مُنذِرِينَ ۝٣ فِيهَا يُفۡرَقُ كُلُّ أَمۡرٍ حَكِيمٍ ۝٤ أَمۡرٗا مِّنۡ عِندِنَآۚ إِنَّا كُنَّا مُرۡسِلِينَ ۝٥﴾

"We sent it down on a night full of blessings; surely We have ever been warning (humankind since their creation). In that night every affair is identified and made distinct for wise purposes, As a command issued from Our Presence; surely We have ever been sending Messengers (from among the angels and human beings to convey Our decrees and guide)."

This meaning is in harmony with numerous narrations which state: On that night, the affairs and destinies of humanity are determined - sustenance, illnesses, the end of lives, and other affairs are made distinct and clear.

This matter of course does not contradict the free-will which humanity has been given because Divine Wisdom is carried out by the angels based on humanities' efficiencies and abilities on the level of their faith and virtues, and purity of their intentions and actions - meaning that everyone is sustained with what they deserve, or in other words, the path is paved by the person themselves; and not only does this belief not contradict one's 'free-will,' but rather it emphasizes it.

2. Some scholars have also mentioned that this Night is called the Night of *Qadr* because it is of immense importance and honour beyond comprehension, like what is stated in Sūrah al-Ḥajj (22), verse 74:

﴿مَا قَدَرُوا اللَّهَ حَقَّ قَدْرِهِ﴾

"They do not regard Allah with the regard that is due to Him."

3. Some others have said that it is called the Night of *Qadr* because the Noble Quran, with all its magnificence and splendour, descended to the magnificent Messenger of Allah ﷺ by means of His magnificent angel.
4. Another meaning is that it is a Night in which the descent of the Quran was appointed.
5. Yet another meaning is that the person who keeps vigil on that Night will obtain a grand rank.
6. The final meaning is that so many angels descend on that Night that the expanse of the Earth becomes restricted and does not have enough room for all of them, thus one of the meanings of *'taqdīr'* (which comes from the same root as *qadr*) is 'restricting' - just as we see in Sūrah al-Ṭalāq (65), verse 7:

﴿...وَمَنْ قُدِرَ عَلَيْهِ رِزْقُهُ فَلْيُنفِقْ مِمَّا آتَاهُ اللَّهُ...﴾

> "...and let the one whose provision has been **tightened** (or **restricted**) spend out of what Allah has given them..."

The combination of all these commentaries on the vast meaning of the Night of *Qadr* is quite possible, however, the first commentary is the most appropriate, commonly known, and more accepted one.

When is the Night of Qadr?

No doubt that the Night of *Qadr* is during the month of Ramaḍān since several verses of the Quran attest to this very fact. From one angle, we see in Sūrah al-Baqarah (2), verse 185 where it says:

﴿شَهْرُ رَمَضَانَ الَّذِي أُنزِلَ فِيهِ الْقُرْآنُ...﴾

> "(The) Month of Ramaḍān is the one in which the Quran was sent down..."

In the chapter under discussion, Sūrah al-Qadr, we read:

﴿إِنَّا أَنزَلْنَاهُ فِي لَيْلَةِ الْقَدْرِ﴾

"Surely, We sent it (the Quran) down on the Night of Ordainment."

But which night during the month of Ramaḍān does this refer to? In this regard, many commentators and opinions have been stated about which night it actually is, and these include the following: 1ˢᵗ, 17ᵗʰ, 19ᵗʰ, 21ˢᵗ, 23ʳᵈ, 27ᵗʰ, or 29ᵗʰ. However, the most popular in the narrations is that it is one of the last ten nights of the month of Ramaḍān, emphasizing on the 21ˢᵗ or 23ʳᵈ night. We also read in a narration which states that the Noble Prophet would keep vigil and be busy praying all of the nights during the last ten nights of this sacred month.

A narration from Imām Jaʿfar al-Ṣādiq denotes that the Night of Ordainment is either the 21ˢᵗ or 23ʳᵈ night of the month of Ramaḍān; and when a person insisted and asked that if one cannot worship on both nights, then which one should they choose, to which the Imām replied:

$$\text{مَا أَيْسَرَ لَيْلَتَيْنِ فِيمَا تَطْلُبُ}$$

"How easy is it (to spend) two nights for what you seek!"⁸¹

However, in numerous narrations from the Ahlul Bayt, the 23ʳᵈ night is emphasized, while the narrations of the Sunni scholars tend towards the 27ᵗʰ night.

Further, a narration from Imām Jaʿfar al-Ṣādiq also says:

$$\text{أَلتَّقْدِيرُ فِي لَيْلَةِ الْقَدْرِ تِسْعَةُ عَشَرَ وَالإِبْرَامُ فِي لَيْلَةِ إِحَدى وَعِشْرِينَ}$$
$$\text{وَالإِمْضَاءُ فِي لَيْلَةِ ثَلَاثُ وَعِشْرِينَ.}$$

"Determining the proportions *(taqdīr)* is in the Night of Ordainment - the 19ᵗʰ night; its confirmation *(ibrām)* is on

---

⁸¹ *Tafsīr Nūr al-Thaqalayn*, Vol. 5, Pg. 625, Ḥadīth 58.

> the 21st night; and its signing off *(imḍā)* is on the 23rd night."[82]

Therefore, through this tradition we see that all the explanations have been combined - however, a kind of mystic ambiguity still covers the Night of Ordainment, and the reason for this will be discussed later.

Why Keep the Date Hidden?

Many commentators believe that the Night of *Qadr* being hidden among the nights of the year, or during the nights of the month of Ramaḍān is because people should consider all the nights to be important, just like Allah ﷻ has:

1. Hidden His pleasure in various kinds of obedience and worship, such that people practice all of them.
2. Hidden His wrath in sinning in general, so that people avoid all kinds of sin.
3. Hidden His special friendship among all of humanity so that everyone will be honoured.
4. Concealed the supplication to which He listens (and will directly accept and fulfill) among all supplications, so that one will refer to the various supplications when they want to call upon Him.
5. Hidden His Greatest Name, among His universal Names so that people will remember and call upon Him with all of His Divine Names.
6. Kept hidden the time of death so that humankind will always be prepared.

And indeed, these are all fitting philosophies!

---

[82] *Tafsīr Nūr al-Thaqalayn*, Vol. 5, Pg. 626, Ḥadīth 62.

Night of Qadr in Previous Communities

The verses of this chapter apparently show that the Night of *Qadr* was not specifically restricted to the time of the descent of the Quran and the period of the call of the Messenger of Islam ﷺ, but rather that it repeats annually until the end of this world. The application of the verb *'tanazzala'* in this chapter - which is in the future tense and indicates an act of continuity - and by using the phrase: 'Peace it is until the rising of the dawn' which is a nounal phrase, shows perpetuity, and both conform to this idea.

In addition, there are also many other narrations which reach to a level of *'tawātur'* - a frequency of successive transmission - which also attest to this belief.

Now, a question may arise whether the previous communities also had such a night, or not?

Many narrations clearly indicate that this is a Divine blessing which has only been endowed to Muslims. In a tradition, the Noble Prophet ﷺ is narrated to have said:

إِنَّ اللّٰهَ وَهَبَ لِأُمَّتِي لَيْلَةَ الْقَدْرِ لَمْ يُعْطِهَا مَنْ كَانَ قَبْلَهُمْ

> "Surely, Allah has bestowed on my community the Night of Ordainment which He did not give to any of those (people) who were before them."[83]

In commenting on the above verses, there are some other narrations that indicate the same opinion.

[83] *Tafsīr Durr al-Manthūr*, Vol. 6, Pg. 371.

Better than One Thousand Months?

Apparently, this Night being better than a thousand months is for the value of worshipping and keeping vigil on that Night. The narrations on the virtue of the Night of *Qadr* and the merits of worship in it are abundantly mentioned in the books of both the Shīʿas and Sunnis who confirm this meaning. Furthermore, the descent of the Quran on that Night and the descent of the Divine blessings and grace in it causes the Night to be even better than a thousand months!

A tradition says that Imām Jaʿfar al-Ṣādiq ﷺ told ʿAlī ibn Abū Hamzah al-Thumālī: "Seek the virtue of the Night of *Qadr* on the 21st and 23rd night and say one hundred *rakʿat ṣalāt* on either of them, and if you can, then keep vigil on both of the nights until the break of dawn and perform ritual bathing *(ghusl)* therein."

Abū Hamzah says that he asked Imām Jaʿfar al-Ṣādiq ﷺ that if he cannot pray that many prayers in the standing position, what should he do, so the Imām replied: "Then pray in the sitting position."

Again, he asked that if he cannot do that, then what should he do, to which the Imām answered: "Pray in bed, and it does not matter if you sleep a little at the beginning of the night and then begin praying, because in the month of Ramaḍān, the gates of Paradise are open, the devils are bound in chains, and the deeds of the believers are accepted. What a great month the month of Ramaḍān is!"[84]

Why Reveal the Quran on That Night?

This Book was revealed on the Night of *Qadr* because the destiny of humanity for the next year is determined based on our

---

[84] *Tafsīr Nūr al-Thaqalayn*, Vol. 5, Pg. 625, Ḥadīth 58 (summarized).

worthiness, and thus, we should keep vigil the entire night and repent for our sins, practice self-perfection, and turn towards Allah ﷻ to gain a great share of an even higher amount of worthiness, and to attain His vast mercy.

We need to be aware of the moments in which our fate is formed and not spend the time in spiritual negligence, otherwise our destiny will be nothing but regret.

Since the Quran is a book of forging one's destiny and can lead to the path of happiness and guidance for all of humanity, it should be sent down on the Night of *Qadr* - a Night of determining the fates of humankind. What a nice connection there is between the Quran and the Night of *Qadr,* and how meaningful their relationship is to one another!

Is the Night of Qadr the Same Night Globally?

We know that the beginning of the lunar month is not the same in all parts of the world; for example, in one region today it may be the first day of a month, but in another region that same day may be the second day of the month. Therefore, the Night of *Qadr* cannot be a definite night in the year for everyone because the 23rd of a month in Mecca may be the 22nd of that month in Iran or Iraq; but each of them as a rule have a Night of *Qadr* for themselves according to the region they live in.

Does this fact fit with the meaning understood from the verses and narrations that state that the Night of *Qadr* is a definite Night?

The answer to this question will be clear when we consider the following point:

The words 'rotation' and 'revolution' mean a similar thing. But in describing the Earth's movements, each word is used for a different kind of motion.

Revolution refers to the motion of the Earth in its yearly orbit around the Sun. Rotation refers to the spinning around of the Earth on its own axis every 24 hours in relation to the Sun. It is 24 hours from high noon on one day to high noon on the next day. In its rotation on its axis, half of the surface of the Earth is towards the sun, whereupon it is day, and on the opposite part at the same time, it is night.

The night, which is regarded as the shade for the Earth, itself turns around in a complete circle for 24 hours all over the Earth. Therefore, the Night of *Qadr* may be a Night of a complete circle around the Earth, meaning that for 24 hours, where darkness covers all the points of the Earth, itself is the Night of *Qadr* whose beginning starts from one point, and ends at another point.

Fāṭima al-Zahrā' is the Night of Qadr[85]

Muḥammad ibn Qāsim says that Imām Jaʿfar al-Ṣādiq ﷺ said:

﴿إِنَّا أَنْزَلْنَاهُ فِي لَيْلَةِ الْقَدْرِ﴾ أَللَّيْلَةُ فَاطِمَةُ وَالْقَدْرُ اللهُ. فَمَنْ عَرَفَ فَاطِمَةَ حَقَّ مَعْرِفَتِهَا فَقَدْ أَدْرَكَ لَيْلَةَ الْقَدْرِ. وَإِنَّمَا سُمِّيَتْ فَاطِمَةَ لِأَنَّ الْخَلْقَ فُطِمُوا عَنْ مَعْرِفَتِهَا.

"﴾Indeed, We send it (the Quran) down on the Night of *Qadr* ﴿. The in-depth *(ta'wīl)* interpretation of 'The Night *(al-Layl)*' is Fāṭima, and the in-depth *(ta'wīl)* interpretation of *'al-Qadr'* is Allah. Therefore, a person who has truly grasped a deep understanding of Fāṭima (and who she is) has witnessed and experienced the Night of *Qadr*. Indeed, Fāṭima was called by this name because the creations have

---

[85] This section has been translated from the book, *Manifestation of the Divine Light,* written by Shaykh ʿAlī Saʿādat Parvar.

been prevented from truly knowing and having a deep understanding of Fāṭima (we are not able to know her true stature with Allah)."[86]

How is Fāṭima al-Zahrā' ﷺ al-Qadr?

If we accept the fact that the Noble Quran descended on to the heart of the Messenger of Allah ﷺ on the Night of *Qadr* in one instance and not in portions, like the researchers from amongst the exegetes of the Noble Quran have stated, then the challenges which this tradition and other such traditions pose in regard to the Blessed Night *(Laylatul Mubāraka),* and the ambiguities on how both of these are related and refer directly about Lady Fāṭima al-Zahrā' ﷺ will become resolved:

﴿إِنَّا أَنْزَلْنَاهُ فِي لَيْلَةٍ مُبَارَكَةٍ...﴾

"Indeed, We have sent it down on the blessed Night..."[87]

This is the case because the Noble Quran which descended upon the heart of the Messenger of Allah ﷺ is not the written, apparent, physical Quran which we have today; rather, it is the reality *(ḥaqīqah)* of the Quran for which the Prophet ﷺ enjoys the station of *Divine Celestial Light (Maqām-e Nūrāniyat)* and *Complete Authority (Wilāyat-e Muṭlaqah),* which is a station of absolute authority and is not autonomous with that of the Divine Authority of Allah ﷻ, which the Prophet ﷺ, in the form of a human being and possessing his humanistic element has been referred to in these verses with the word 'Night.'

Thus, by keeping in mind this point that the Prophet of Islam ﷺ, with his status of having the **Divine Celestial Light,** and also his possessing the **Complete Authority,** and that he is indeed a manifestation of the reality *(ḥaqīqah)* of the Quran; and in

---

[86] *Tafsīr Durr al-Manthūr,* Vol. 6, Pg. 371.

[87] Quran, Sūrah al-Dukhān (44), verse 3.

addition, that with the blessings of the immaculate leaders - of which Fāṭima al-Zahrā᾽ ﷺ is also considered as being a part of - that they too are all blessed with having the **Divine Celestial Light** and also possessing the **Complete Authority** - which is not separate from that of the Messenger of Allah ﷺ, what problem is there in stating that this meaning can be applied to each and every one of the 14 immaculate ones ﷺ, and that either of these two verses can be interpreted as referring to them!?

Therefore, there is no problem in stating that Fāṭima al-Zahrā᾽ ﷺ is the spiritual interpretation of 'that Night' which has been mentioned in both Sūrah al-Qadr and Sūrah al-Dukhān, and that this great lady - with her **Divine Celestial Light** - is the true reality *(ḥaqīqah)* of the Quran as:

1. She is one of the 14 Immaculate ones.
2. She is at the station of the **Divine Celestial Light**.[88]
3. She is at a similar ranking as the Messenger of Allah ﷺ and the 12 Immaculate and Pure Imāms ﷺ.

From the point of view of her physical creation, she can be referred to as 'the Night.'[89] Thus, it is no problem for us to state that "The spiritual interpretation of 'the Night' is Lady Fāṭima ﷺ, and that the Quran was revealed within her **Spiritual Divine Celestial Light.**"

However, as to why the word *'al-Qadr'* has been related to Allah ﷻ in this tradition, it may be due to the overall universality

---

88 The meaning here is that of the **Spiritual Divine Celestial Light,** and not her creation from Divine Light; the explanation between the difference which exists between these two has been mentioned in the first chapter of the book, *The Manifestation of the Divine Light.* For further explanation, one can refer to section 2 of the book, *The Branches of Martyrdom.*

89 Why the use of the word "Night" and its darkness? The response to this is that the attribute of manifestation of Fāṭima al-Zahrā ﷺ in the face of the Pure Light of Allah ﷻ and the Divine Authority of Allah ﷻ is nothing other than a shadow and obscurity.

of this grand woman, Fāṭima al-Zahrā' ﷺ, being a manifestation of His Titles, Traits, and Essence. The proof of this point and the previous points are contained in part of a tradition which states:

فَمَنْ عَرَفَ فَاطِمَةَ حَقَّ مَعْرِفَتِهَا...

"Therefore, a person who truly recognizes Fāṭima as she deserves to be recognized..."

It is possible that the augmentation of the word 'Night' to the word *'al-Qadr'* - in its apparent reading from the actual words - and its reference to Allah ﷻ in its meaning and interpretation - is done in the genitive ceremonial case. For example, we see in the Quran where the word 'hand' and 'house' are often attributed to Allah ﷻ, and as such we see passages in the Quran which speak about "Allah's Hand" or "The House of Allah."

Fāṭima ﷺ is the Very Night of Divine Decrees

Anyone who really knows and understands Lady Fāṭima ﷺ as she truly is, has understood the Night of Divine Decrees. Very few people know this great lady ﷺ in this way.

Imām Ja'far al-Sadiq ﷺ once said in a tradition recorded in the commentary of Furāt ibn Ibrāhīm, speaking about the meaning of the Quranic verse: "The Night of Divine Decrees (*Laylatul Qadr*) is Fāṭima, therefore whoever knows Fāṭima well has understood the Night of Divine Decrees; and the reason for Fāṭima being named Fāṭima[90] is that humankind has been 'prevented from obtaining her acquaintance' (or knowing her real status)." *(Biḥār al-Anwār)*

---

[90] Fāṭima is from the root *fa-ta-ma*, originally meaning "weaning from milk." Among the reasons which have been mentioned for the appropriate choice of this name for this Lady of Light, the above meaning has also been included.

We know that Quranic verses have a literal meaning and a figurative meaning, and many interpretations within them. Without a doubt, the literal interpretation of Sūrah al-Qadr tells us about a Night in which the Noble Quran descended upon the pure heart of the Prophet ﷺ, and in which the Divine Decrees (destinies) of human beings are ascertained for a year, according to Divine Wisdom. As such, what was said in the tradition above is a figurative interpretation of this chapter's meaning, or a deeper understanding of Sūrah al-Qadr.

What a close relationship there is between the existence of this Lady of Light and the Night of Divine Decrees! Some of the points we can derive from this connection are as follows:

1. The Night of Divine Decrees - the disguised, unknown Night of *Qadr* - is undoubtedly this great Lady, whom the Prophet ﷺ would refer to as a part of his flesh, and reckoned her pleasure to Allah's pleasure, and her anger to Allah's anger. She is also the veiled and unknown just as the Night of *Qadr* is.
2. The Night of *Qadr* is hidden among the nights of the year. The grave of Lady Fāṭima ؏ is also unknown among the graves of the great Personages of Islam ؏. Those who wish to pay their respects to her and enter Medina, visit the shrines of all the other great ones and seek her grave, but only to be unable to find it, will well understand the heavy load of this sorrow.
3. The Night of *Qadr* is better than 1,000 months of worship; and the virtue of worship on that Night is greater than that of a long life of 80 years. The virtue of this great Lady is also greater than thousands upon thousands of virtuous persons, and her rank is more superior than them.
4. The Night of *Qadr* was the Night in which the Quran descended upon the pure heart of the Prophet of Islam ﷺ, and it was a sudden, all-at-once revelation, even

though its gradual descent took over 23 years. The "Night of *Qadr*" may also therefore be named as the "Night of the Descent of Virtue, Perfection, Knowledge, and Wisdom." The being of Lady Fāṭima ﷺ is also a source of luminosity of the guardianship and Imāmate, Divine knowledge, and wisdom. The written or silent Quran *(Quran al-Ṣāmiṭ)* descended on the Night of *Qadr*, but Fāṭima ﷺ is the one from whom 11 speaking Qurans (*Quran al-Nāṭiq*) descended!

5. The Night of *Qadr* is the Night in which, by the command of Allah, the Angels ascertain the destinies of all human beings and present them to the *Walī al-Amr*, the Guardian of His Command. It is a Night of serenity and goodness in its entirety: "Peace, it is until the rising of the dawn." (Sūrah al-Qadr (97), verse 5). The brief life of this Lady of Light was also goodness, soundness, and blessed from the very beginning until the end - and even beyond that - and was given the attention and interest of the Angels.

The close relationship between the Night of *Qadr* and the being of Lady Fāṭima ﷺ deems it necessary for all of us to strive harder to know her and obtain greater benefits from the blessings of her radiance.

O Lord! Bestow on us such a spiritual awakening that we take sufficient benefit from the virtue of the Night of Ordainment.

O Lord! We hope only that our predestined fates are determined based on Your Grace.

O Lord! Do not make us among those who are deprived from this special Night, because it is the worst deprivation.

...So be it, O Lord of all the Worlds.

End of Sūrah al-Qadr

Fāṭima al-Zahrā’ عليها السلام in the Noble Quran

Sūrah al-Kawthar

The Chapter of Abundant Good

This chapter was revealed in Mecca and contains 3 verses

Sūrah al-Kawthar

Contents of Sūrah al-Kawthar

It is commonly held that this chapter was revealed in Mecca, however, there are some scholars who believe that it may have been revealed in Medina. Another opinion states that this chapter was revealed twice - once in Mecca and once in Medina. However, the narrations cited on its revelation attest to the first idea which says that it is a Meccan chapter.

Regarding the occasion of revelation, the following story has been narrated:

ʿĀṣ ibn Wā'il, who was one of the chiefs of the pagans, met Prophet Muḥammad ﷺ as he was coming out of the Sacred Masjid *(Masjid al-Ḥarām).* When ʿĀṣ ibn Wā'il proceeded to speak with the Prophet ﷺ during that brief time, a group of leaders of the Quraysh who were sitting in the Masjid attentively watched him from a distance.

Afterwards, when ʿĀṣ ibn Wā'il entered the Masjid, they asked him: "Who were you speaking to?" He replied: "With the *'abtar'* one."

ʿĀṣ ibn Wā'il used this derogatory word - *abtar* - for the Prophet ﷺ to taunt him, because he knew that the Messenger ﷺ had a son named ʿAbdullāh who died in his infancy, and in the language of the Arabs, a person who had no male offspring was referred to as *'abtar'* - meaning one who has no posterity to follow him. Thus, the Quraysh gave the Noble Prophet ﷺ this nickname after the death of his son.

To condole His beloved Prophet ﷺ, Allah ﷻ revealed this Sūrah with the glad tidings of the greatest amount of grace - *al-Kawthar*

- an abundance of goodness from Allah ﷻ - and how the Prophet's ﷺ opponents will be *'abtar'* or have no posterity.[91]

In summary: The Noble Prophet ﷺ had two male children from his first wife, Khadījah ؑ - one was named Qāsim, and the other one was named Ṭāhir, who was also known as ʿAbdullāh. Both passed away in Mecca, thus the Prophet ﷺ did not have any living son at that time. This tragic event gave the Quraysh an opportunity to hurl insults at the Prophet ﷺ and refer to him as *'abtar'* or one who has no surviving male children.[92]

According to their traditional ways, the ʿArabs gave a great deal of importance to male children and considered the son as being an extension of one's father. Thus, after the death of his two sons, they thought that with the eventual death of the Prophet ﷺ, his mission of spreading Islam would also cease to exist as he had no male children to continue his message, and this pleased the polytheistic ʿArabs greatly!

Through a miraculous message in this chapter, Allah ﷻ replied to these individuals and let them know that: It is the enemies of the Prophet who will be *'abtar'* or cut off in progeny, and that the program of Islam and the Quran will never come to a halt!

The revelation of this Sūrah was in fact, an answer to the enemies of the Apostle of Allah ﷺ to inform them that Islam and the Quran will remain and continue forever. From another point of view, it was also consolation for the Messenger of Allah ﷺ that after he heard this despicable nickname which the enemies gave him, his heart was brought to tranquility through this great news.

---

[91] *Tafsīr Majmaʿ al-Bayān*, Vol. 10, Pg. 549.

[92] The Noble Prophet ﷺ had other male children as well - namely Ibrāhīm, from his wife, Māriyah al-Qibṭiyya, who was born in Medina. Coincidentally, he too passed away before reaching the age of two, and his death also weighed heavily on the heart of the Prophet ﷺ.

Virtue of Studying this Chapter

Regarding the virtue of the recitation of this chapter, a tradition from the Noble Prophet ﷺ says:

مَنْ قَرَأَهَا سَقَاهُ اللهُ مِنْ أَنْهَارِ الْجَنَّةِ وَأُعْطِيَ مِنَ الأَجْرِ بِعَدَدِ كُلِّ قُرْبَانٍ قَرَّبَهُ الْعِبَادُ فِي يَوْمِ عِيدٍ وَيَقْرَبُونَ مِنْ أَهْلِ الْكِتَابِ وَالْمُشْرِكِينَ

> "The person who recites it (Sūrah al-Kawthar), Allah will quench their thirst from the streams of Heaven and will recompense them good rewards, as many as the number of every sacrifice which the servants of Allah make on the day of the Feast of Sacrifice *('Eid al-Qurbān)*, together with those sacrifices which are (performed) from the People of the Book and the polytheists."[93]

The name of this Sūrah, *al-Kawthar*, is taken from the first verse of it.

---

[93] *Tafsīr Majma' al-Bayān*, Vol. 10, Pg. 548.

بِسۡمِ ٱللَّهِ ٱلرَّحۡمَٰنِ ٱلرَّحِيمِ

In the Name of Allah, the All-Compassionate, the All-Merciful

Section One - Verses 1 to 3

﴿إِنَّآ أَعۡطَيۡنَٰكَ ٱلۡكَوۡثَرَ ١ فَصَلِّ لِرَبِّكَ وَٱنۡحَرۡ ٢ إِنَّ شَانِئَكَ هُوَ ٱلۡأَبۡتَرُ ٣﴾

"Surely, We have given you (Muḥammad) abundance of good *(al-Kawthar).* ۞ Therefore, turn to your Lord in prayer and sacrifice. ۞ Indeed, your enemy is the one who will be without (any) offspring."

We have Given You Much Goodness

In this chapter, like what is seen in Sūrah al-Ḍuḥā and Sūrah al-Inshirāḥ, the Noble Prophet ﷺ is the focal point of the address; and one of the prime objectives in all three of these chapters is to grant consolation to the Prophet ﷺ in relation to the continuous painful incidents against him, the numerous taunts of his enemies, and their harsh language towards him.

We first read: ﴿Surely, We have given you (Muḥammad) an abundance of good *(al-Kawthar)*﴾.

The term *'al-kawthar'* is the descriptive case derived from the Arabic word *'kathrah'* which means 'ample goodness or blessings' and those individuals who are extremely generous are also referred to as *'Kawthar.'*

What is al-Kawthar?

It is mentioned in the narrations that: When this chapter was revealed, Prophet Muḥammad ﷺ ascended the pulpit *(mimbar)* and recited it. His companions asked him what it was that Allah ﷻ gave him, and he replied: "It is a stream in Paradise, whiter than milk, clearer than a goblet (made of crystal), and on either side are domes decorated with pearls and rubies."[94]

In a tradition from Imām Jaʿfar al-Ṣādiq ؏, he says: "*Al-Kawthar* is a stream in Paradise which Allah granted to His Prophet in exchange for his infant son, ʿAbdullāh, who passed away during the lifetime of the Prophet."

Some scholars have stated that *'al-Kawthar'* is a 'Pool of Abundance' which belongs to the Prophet ﷺ from where the believers will quench their thirst when they arrive in Paradise.[95]

Other opinions of *'al-Kawthar'* include the following:

- Some have commented on it as being 'Prophecy.'
- Others mention that it is the Quran.
- Another opinion is that it refers to an abundance of companions and followers of the Prophet ﷺ.
- Yet another interpretation is that it refers to the abundance of descendants - all of whom will come from his daughter, Fāṭima al-Zahrā' ؏ - and will increase to such an extent that it will be impossible to count them. They not only exist today, but in fact will continue to remain until the end of time as reminders of the Noble Prophet ﷺ.
- Some have also commented on this term referring to 'intercession,' and narrate a tradition from Imām Jaʿfar al-Ṣādiq ؏ in this regard.[96]

---

[94] *Tafsīr Majmaʿ al-Bayān*, Vol. 10, Pg. 549.
[95] Ibid.
[96] Ibid.

Even the Sunnī scholar, Fakhr al-Dīn al-Rāzī has narrated fifteen different narrations on the meaning of *'al-Kawthar,'* however, most of them are merely statements of the clear examples of this broad concept, because as was mentioned before, *'al-Kawthar'* means 'goodness and blessings in abundance,' and we know that Allah, the Grand, granted the Noble Prophet ﷺ so many blessings such that each of the ones mentioned above are clear examples of them.

There are many other explanations that may be cited as commentaries for this verse, however we will not mention them here.

All the Divine gifts granted to Prophet Muḥammad ﷺ in every aspect - such as the victories in his expeditions against his enemies; the scholars of his community who in every era and age guard the illuminated torch of Islam and the Quran, and carry it throughout the world, etc. - all in all are contained in this 'abundance of goodness.'

It should not be forgotten that Allah ﷻ revealed these verses to His Prophet's blessed heart at a time when the manifestations of these 'abundance of good' had not yet appeared. It was a miraculous piece of news that he was informed about which was to transpire in the near and remote future to confirm the legitimacy of the Noble Prophet ﷺ.

This great blessing and the 'abundance of good' needs to have a lofty level of thanks given to Allah ﷻ, although creatures can never entirely thank the Creator for His blessings because even the ability to be thankful is another blessing from Him which needs thanks. Therefore, Allah ﷻ says: ﴾Thus, turn towards your Lord in prayer and (offer the) sacrifice﴿.

He is the One who grants these blessings, therefore prayer, worship, and sacrifice - which is also a kind of worship in itself -

has no meaning unless it is done solely for the sake of Allah ﷻ, particularly regarding the meaning of the term 'Lord' which indicates the constancy of grace and providence.

Briefly it can be stated that: 'worship' - whether it be in the form of *ṣalāt* or making a sacrifice of an animal - is only the Lord's and Benefactor's privilege, and it is exclusively for the Pure Supreme Being - Allah ﷻ - to be directed towards.

This portion of the verse refers to the behaviour of the pagans who used to prostrate and sacrifice animals to the idols, while they knew their thanks for all the blessings that they had been given truly belonged only to Allah ﷻ, and the phrase 'your Lord' used in this verse, is clear evidence for the necessity of pure intentions in all acts of worship.

Many commentators believe that the meaning of *ṣalāt* in this verse is the *ṣalāt* on the Day of the Feast of Sacrifice *('Eid al-Qurbān) and* making the sacrifice of an animal on that day. However, the meaning of the verse is general in its scope and inclusive of many other types of prayers, even though *ṣalāt* and the sacrifice of that Day are clear examples of this term.

Perhaps the use of the term 'offer sacrifice' which comes from the root *'na-ḥa-ra'* and is specific to the process of slaughtering a camel has been employed because among all the animals which can be slaughtered on the Day of *'Eid al-Qurbān* and in general, the camel is the best of them. Among the early community of Muslims, that they had a great fondness of slaughtering and eating camel meat, and slaughtering a camel was not possible without a show of generosity due to its great worth and value.

Here are two more commentaries which have been offered on the above verse:

1. An implied meaning of the phrase *'wanḥar'* is 'to face the *qiblah* (the *Ka'bah)'* when performing the *ṣalāt*. This interpretation is given because the word *'naḥar'* originally meant the 'throat,' and then later the Arabs used it to mean the 'act of standing in front of anything.'

2. Another meaning of 'wanḥar' is the 'raising of the hands up to the face and ears when pronouncing the *'takbīr'* (to begin the *ṣalāt).'* In a tradition, we read that when this chapter was revealed, the Noble Prophet ﷺ asked Jibrā'īl ؑ: "What is this *'nuḥaryah'* that my Lord has commissioned me to do?" Jibrā'īl ؑ replied: "This is not *'nuḥaryah;'* rather, Allah has commanded you to raise your hands at the beginning of prayer when you say *'Allahu Akbar,'* and every time when you are going to perform *rukūʿ* or *sajdah* and after that action (raise your hands), because our *ṣalāt* and that of the angels in the seven heavens is exactly like this. Everything has an adornment, and the adornment of prayer is raising the hands at the time of saying *'Allahu Akbar.'* [97]

In another tradition, this one from Imām Jaʿfar al-Ṣādiq ؑ who on the commentary of this verse, indicated with his hands and said: "The meaning of this verse is that you raise your hands in such a way that your palms face towards the *qiblah* (the direction of the Kaʿbah)."[98]

However, the first commentary given is the most appropriate one regarding what this verse means, since its meaning was to negate the actions of the idolaters who used to perform acts of worship - such as sacrificing animals - for other than Allah ﷻ.

However, with this said, there is also no problem in combining all of these meanings together; and in particular, there are many narrations about raising the hands at the time of saying *'Allahu Akbar,'* and there are traditions in the books of the Shīʿa and the Ahl al-Sunnah in this regard, therefore this verse can have a vast meaning that it covers all of them.

---

[97] *Tafsīr Majmaʿ al-Bayān*, Vol. 10, Pg. 550.

[98] Ibid., Pg. 548.

In the last verse of this short chapter, keeping in mind the taunts made by the chiefs of the pagans towards the Noble Prophet ﷺ, we read: ﴿Surely your enemy is the one who will be without offspring﴾.

The term 'enemy' is derived from the word *'shana'ān'* which means 'enmity, spitefulness, and bad manners;' thus, the word *'shānī'* or 'enemy' is the 'one who possesses these characteristics.'

It is worthy to note that the word *'abtar'* originally meant 'an animal whose tail is cut off,' and the enemies of Islam taunted the final Prophet ﷺ by using this word.

The usage of the term *'shānī'* clearly shows that in their desire to express their enmity towards the Messenger ﷺ, these people did not even display the smallest amount of respect or dignity - meaning that their enmity was interwoven with hard-heartedness and the use of such shameful words! The Quran retorted to such individuals and told them: "It is actually **you** who have this characteristic (and will be cut off of your posterity), **not** the Noble Prophet!"

In addition, just as has been mentioned in regard to the history of revelation of this chapter, the Quraysh were waiting for the death of the Prophet ﷺ to transpire as they felt that with his departure from this world, and since he had no son to inherit his position, the dissolution of Islam would happen. But the Quran, consoling the final Messenger ﷺ told him that it is not him who will be without offspring, but rather the lineage of his enemies are the ones which will not continue!

Fāṭima al-Zahrā᾽ ﷺ and al-Kawthar

It was said earlier that *'al-Kawthar'* has a vast, inclusive meaning which is 'goodness in abundance' and the examples are many.

Many scholars of the Shīʿa school believe that one of the clearest examples of this word is the auspicious existence of Fāṭima al-Zahrāʾ ﷺ, because the occasion of revelation of this verse indicates that the enemies accused the Noble Prophet ﷺ of being without offspring to which the Quran replied: ﴾Surely, (O Muḥammad) We have given you abundance of good *(al-Kawthar)*﴿.

From this verse we understand that this 'abundance of good' is that very special, Lady Fāṭima al-Zahrāʾ ﷺ.

In addition, this verse implies that not only is it the physical and biological offspring of the Prophet ﷺ which will increase, rather it is the abundant number of offspring which will be scattered throughout the world that will continue the religion and will be responsible for the preservation of all the values of Islam and continue to convey it to future generations!

This is not only limited to the Immaculate Imāms of the Ahlul Bayt ﷺ who have a literal number that we can enumerate (twelve), rather it is the thousands and thousands of children of Lady Fāṭima ﷺ who have spread around the entire globe from whom so many great scholars, scientists, writers, exegetists, jurists, narrators of the Prophet's sayings and leaders have come from - individuals who have left outstanding works and unmatched fame in this world, and have protected Islam with their selfless giving of themselves, their endless efforts, and their hard work and devotion.

Here, we encounter a remarkably interesting discussion from Fakhr al-Dīn al-Rāzī, who along with other commentators on *'al-Kawthar,'* says: "The third statement of the meaning of this chapter is that it was revealed to reject those who criticized the Noble Prophet ﷺ for his lack of progeny. Therefore, the meaning of this chapter is that Allah ﷻ will give him a generation which will remain throughout all the ages. Imagine how many members, lovers, and followers of the Ahlul Bayt ﷺ have been martyred, yet we still see that the world is replete with them, whereas the Umayyads - who were the staunch enemies of Islam - are completely extinct and there remains no mentionable figure in the world who trace their lineage back to them. Then behold and see how many of the great men of leadership such as al-Bāqir, al-Ṣādiq, al-Riḍā, and *Nafs al-Zakīyyah*,[99] etc... are found among them (that holy household)!"[100]

The Miracle of this Chapter

This chapter contains three important miraculous predictions:

1. On one hand, it informs the Prophet ﷺ about the glad tidings of an 'abundance of good.' Although the verb *'a'ṭaynā'* is in the past tense form, it may be considered as meaning the present and future which has been stated in the form of the past tense; and this 'abundance of good' encompasses all victories and successes that were obtained later by the Noble Prophet ﷺ, however, which were not predictable in Mecca at the time of the revelation of this chapter.
2. On the other hand, the chapter foretells that the final Messenger of Allah ﷺ will not be without posterity, and his generations and descendants will exist abundantly all over the world.
3. The third thing which this chapter foretells is that the enemies of the Prophet ﷺ will be *'abtar'* - without posterity. This too actually happened, and those enemies were so rooted out that no trace of their generations can be seen today. We see that today, tribes such as the Umayyads and Abbasids, who opposed the

[99] *Nafs al-Zakīyyah* is another name for Muḥammad ibn 'Abdullāh, the grandson of Imām Ḥasan al-Mujtabā ﷺ who was martyred by Manṣūr al-Dawānīqī in 145 AH.

[100] *Tafsīr al-Kabīr*, Vol. 32, Pg. 124.

Prophet ﷺ and his prophecy - who enjoyed such a population in the past - today their families and children are not present anywhere, set asides even be counted!

Allah ﷻ and the Plural Pronoun

It is noteworthy to mention that here and in many other verses of the Noble Quran, Allah ﷻ introduces Himself by the first-person plural pronoun and uses 'We' such as in the first verse of this sūrah where He says: "We have given you an abundance of good *(al-Kawthar).*"

This expression and similar ones serve to emphasize His greatness and power. When the great and powerful people speak, they not only speak for themselves, but also announce things through their representatives. This allusion underscores the power and magnificence of having subordinates who carry out His commands.

In the verse under discussion, the term *'inna'* is another emphasis on this meaning, and the phrase *'a'ṭaynāka'* (أَعْطَيْنَاكَ)- "We have **granted** you" rather than *'ā'taynāka'* (آتَيْنَاكَ) which means 'We have **given** you' is evidence to the fact that **Allah ﷻ has awarded** Prophet Muḥammad ﷺ "*al-Kawthar*" which itself is a great glad tiding to the Messenger ﷺ in order to keep his heart serene and tranquil, and aloof from annoyance resulting from the nonsensical remarks of the enemies. Furthermore, it was comfort for him to know that Allah ﷻ is his support, and that He is the source of all welfare and grace in abundance.

O Lord! Do not deprive us from the blessings of that 'abundance of good' that You granted to Your Prophet ﷺ.

O Lord! You know that we genuinely love Your Prophet and his Pure Progeny ﷺ; therefore, include us among their ranks.

O Sustainer of all! The greatness of Your Prophet and his way are truly magnificent, so day by day, please increase this magnificence, honour and splendor.

...So be it, O Lord of all the Worlds.

End of Sūrah al-Kawthar

Various Ziyārāt for Fāṭima al-Zahrā' ﷺ

Translated by Badr Shahin
with Edits by Arifa Hudda and Saleem Bhimji

While standing in the area between the Noble Prophet's tomb and *mimbar* - a place described as a Garden of Paradise - *al-Rawdah*, you may pay your respects to Lady Fāṭima al-Zahrā' ﷺ, although there is a disagreement about the place of her tomb. Some say that she was buried in *al-Rawdah*; others say she was buried in her own house; while others say that she was buried in the cemetery known as *Jannatul Baqī'*. However, most of our scholars agree that she should be visited within the area of *al-Rawdah*, although to visit her at all three of these places is preferable.

Ziyārah One

When you stand for the *ziyārah* of Lady Fāṭima al-Zahrā' ﷺ, recite the following:

بِسْمِ اللّٰهِ الرَّحْمٰنِ الرَّحِيمِ

"In the Name of Allah, the All-Compassionate, the All-Merciful

يَا مُـمْتَحَنَةُ.

O the carefully examined one.

إِمْتَحَنَكِ اللّٰهُ الَّذِي خَلَقَكِ قَبْلَ أَنْ يَـخْلُقَكِ،

Allah had tried you before He created you (for this worldly life),

فَوَجَدَكِ لِـمَا امْتَحَنَكِ صَابِرَةً.

And thus, He found you successfully enduring in that trial.[101]

---

[101] For a detailed understanding of this passage of the visitation, please

وَزَعَمْنَا أَنَّا لَكِ أَوْلِيَآءٌ وَمُصَدِّقُونَ،

We declare that we are your followers and believers,

وَصَابِرُونَ لِكُلِّ مَا أَتَانَا بِهِ أَبُوكِ صَلَّى اللّٰهُ عَلَيْهِ وَآلِهِ،

And patient with all that has been conveyed to us by your father - peace of Allah be upon him and his household,

وَأَتَـىٰ بِهِ وَصِيُّهُ.

And all that which his successor (Imām ʿAlī ibn Abī Ṭālib) brought.

فَإِنَّا نَسْأَلُكِ إِنْ كُنَّا صَدَّقْنَاكِ،

Thus, we ask you that if we have genuinely believed in you,

إِلَّا أَلْـحَقْتِنَا بِتَصْدِيقِنَا لَـهُمْ،

That you may include us with those who believe in them all (the Prophet's successors),

لِنُبَشِّرَ أَنْفُسَنَا بِأَنَّا قَدْ طَهُرْنَا بِوِلَايَتِكِ.

So that we may grant ourselves the glad tidings that we have been purified on account of our loyalty towards you."

It is recommended to also add the following:

أَلسَّلَامُ عَلَيْكِ يَا بِنْتَ رَسُولِ اللّٰهِ.

"Peace be upon you, O daughter of the Messenger of Allah.

---

refer to the following booklet:
http://al-mubin.org/attachments/558_TheDivineTestofFatimaZahra.pdf

أَلسَّلَامُ عَلَيْكِ يَا بِنْتَ نَبِيِّ اللّٰهِ.

Peace be upon you, O daughter of the Prophet of Allah.

أَلسَّلَامُ عَلَيْكِ يَا بِنْتَ حَبِيبِ اللّٰهِ.

Peace be upon you, O daughter of the most beloved of Allah.

أَلسَّلَامُ عَلَيْكِ يَا بِنْتَ خَلِيلِ اللّٰهِ.

Peace be upon you, O daughter of the close friend of Allah.

أَلسَّلَامُ عَلَيْكِ يَا بِنْتَ صَفِيِّ اللّٰهِ.

Peace be upon you, O daughter of the chosen one of Allah.

أَلسَّلَامُ عَلَيْكِ يَا بِنْتَ أَمِينِ اللّٰهِ.

Peace be upon you, O daughter of the trustee of Allah.

أَلسَّلَامُ عَلَيْكِ يَا بِنْتَ خَيْرِ خَلْقِ اللّٰهِ.

Peace be upon you, O daughter of the best of Allah's creations.

أَلسَّلَامُ عَلَيْكِ يَا بِنْتَ أَفْضَلِ أَنْبِيَآءِ اللّٰهِ وَرُسُلِهِ وَمَلآئِكَتِهِ.

Peace be upon you, O daughter of the best among the Prophets of Allah, His Messengers, and His Angels.

أَلسَّلَامُ عَلَيْكِ يَا بِنْتَ خَيْرِ الْبَرِيَّةِ.

Peace be upon you, O daughter of the best of created beings.

أَلسَّلَامُ عَلَيْكِ يَا سَيِّدَةَ نِسَآءِ الْعَالَمِينَ مِنَ الْأَوَّلِينَ وَالْآخِرِينَ.

Peace be upon you, O the Leader of all women of the world, from the first to the last generations.

أَلسَّلَامُ عَلَيْكِ يَا زَوْجَةَ وَلِيِّ اللهِ وَخَيْرِ الْخَلْقِ بَعْدَ رَسُولِ اللهِ.

Peace be upon you, O the wife of the guardian of (the message of) Allah and the best of all created beings after the Messenger of Allah.

أَلسَّلَامُ عَلَيْكِ يَا أُمَّ الْحَسَنِ وَالْحُسَيْنِ،

Peace be upon you, O the mother of Ḥasan and Ḥusayn,

سَيِّدَيْ شَبَابِ أَهْلِ الْجَنَّةِ.

The two masters of the youth of Paradise.

أَلسَّلَامُ عَلَيْكِ أَيَّتُهَا الصِّدِّيقَةُ الشَّهِيدَةُ.

Peace be upon you, O the Veracious *(al-Ṣiddīqa)*, the Martyred *(al-Shahīda)*.

أَلسَّلَامُ عَلَيْكِ أَيَّتُهَا الرَّضِيَّةُ الْمَرْضِيَّةُ.

Peace be upon you, O the Content *(al-Raḍīyya)*, the Pleased *(al-Marḍiyya)*.

أَلسَّلَامُ عَلَيْكِ أَيَّتُهَا الْفَاضِلَةُ الزَّكِيَّةُ.

Peace be upon you, O the Virtuous *(al-Fāḍhila)*, the Pure *(al-Zakiyya)*.

أَلسَّلَامُ عَلَيْكِ أَيَّتُهَا الْحَوْرَآءُ الإِنْسِيَّةُ.

Peace be upon you, O the Paradisiacal human being *(al-Ḥawrā' al-Insiyya)*.

أَلسَّلَامُ عَلَيْكِ أَيَّتُهَا التَّقِيَّةُ النَّقِيَّةُ.

Peace be upon you, O the Pious *(al-Taqiyya)*, the Immaculate *(al-Naqiyya)*.

أَلسَّلَامُ عَلَيْكِ أَيَّتُهَا الْـمُحَدَّثَةُ الْعَلِيمَةُ.

Peace be upon you, O the one whom the angels spoke to *(al-Muḥaddatha)*, the Knowledgeable *(al-ʿAlīma).*

أَلسَّلَامُ عَلَيْكِ أَيَّتُهَا الْـمَظْلُومَةُ الْـمَغْصُوبَةُ.

Peace be upon you, O the Oppressed lady *(al-Maẓlūma)* whose rights were usurped *(al-Maghṣūba).*

أَلسَّلَامُ عَلَيْكِ أَيَّتُهَا الْـمُضْطَهَدَةُ الْـمَقْهُورَةُ.

Peace be upon you, O the Persecuted *(al-Muḍṭahada)*, the Maltreated *(al-Maqhūra).*

أَلسَّلَامُ عَلَيْكِ يَا فَاطِمَةُ بِنْتَ رَسُولِ اللّٰهِ،

Peace be upon you, O Fāṭima, daughter of the Messenger of Allah,

وَرَحْمَةُ اللّٰهِ وَبَرَكَاتُهُ.

And may the mercy and blessings of Allah (be upon you).

صَلَّى اللّٰهُ عَلَيْكِ،

May Allah bless you,

وَعَلىٰ رُوحِكِ وَبَدَنِكِ،

And your soul and your body.

أَشْهَدُ أَنَّكِ مَضَيْتِ عَلىٰ بَيِّنَةٍ مِنْ رَبِّكِ.

I bear witness that you spent your (entire) life with full awareness of your duties towards your Lord.

وَأَنَّ مَنْ سَرَّكِ فَقَدْ سَرَّ رَسُولَ اللّٰهِ صَلَّى اللّٰهُ عَلَيْهِ وَآلِهِ.

And (I bear witness) that one who pleases you, has pleased the Messenger of Allah - blessings of Allāh be upon him and his family.

وَمَنْ جَفَاكِ فَقَدْ جَفَا رَسُولَ اللّٰهِ صَلَّى اللّٰهُ عَلَيْهِ وَآلِهِ.

And one who has betrayed you has indeed betrayed the Messenger of Allah - blessings of Allāh be upon him and his family.

وَمَنْ آذَاكِ فَقَدْ آذَى رَسُولَ اللّٰهِ صَلَّى اللّٰهُ عَلَيْهِ وَآلِهِ.

And one who hurts you, has hurt the Messenger of Allah - blessings of Allāh be upon him and his family.

وَمَنْ وَصَلَكِ فَقَدْ وَصَلَ رَسُولَ اللّٰهِ صَلَّى اللّٰهُ عَلَيْهِ وَآلِهِ.

And one who associates with you, has associated with the Messenger of Allah - blessings of Allāh be upon him and his family.

وَمَنْ قَطَعَكِ فَقَدْ قَطَعَ رَسُولَ اللّٰهِ صَلَّى اللّٰهُ عَلَيْهِ وَآلِهِ.

And one who breaks off ties with you, has broken off ties with the Messenger of Allah - blessings of Allāh be upon him and his family.

لِأَنَّكِ بِضْعَةٌ مِنْهُ،

This is because you are an inseparable part of him (the Prophet),

وَرُوحُهُ الَّذِي بَيْنَ جَنْبَيْهِ.

And you are his soul with which he lives.

أُشْهِدُ اللّٰهَ وَرُسُلَهُ وَمَلَآئِكَتَهُ،

I ask Allah, His Messengers, and His angels to be the witnesses,

أَنِّي رَاضٍ عَمَّنْ رَضِيتِ عَنْهُ،

That indeed I am pleased with the one you are pleased with,

سَاخِطٌ عَلىٰ مَنْ سَخِطْتِ عَلَيْهِ،

And I am displeased with the one you are displeased with,

مُتَبَرِّئٌ مِـمَّنْ تَبَرَّأْتِ مِنْهُ،

And I disavow the one whomsoever you disavow,

مُوَالٍ لِـمَنْ وَالَيْتِ،

And I am loyal to the one whom you support,

مُعَادٍ لِـمَنْ عَادَيْتِ،

And I am an enemy of the one whom you betake as an enemy,

مُبْغِضٌ لِـمَنْ أَبْغَضْتِ،

And I am hateful to the one whom you hate,

مُحِبٌّ لِـمَنْ أَحْبَبْتِ.

And I like the one whom you like.

وَكَفىٰ بِاللّٰهِ شَهِيدًا وَحَسِيبًا،

And verily, Allah is Sufficient as a Witness, and a Reckoner,

وَجَازِيًا وَمُثِيبًا.

And a Punisher, and a Rewarder.

You may then pray to Almighty Allah ﷻ to send blessings upon the Noble Prophet ﷺ and the Imāms ﵈.

Ziyārah Two

Among the recommended acts on the third of *Jumādī al-Ākhir* - the martyrdom day of Lady Fāṭima al-Zahrā' ﷺ - another form of *ziyārah* for her has also been cited by some scholars whose statements are like the statements of the *ziyārah* that was quoted from Shaykh al-Ṭūsī. However, the complete form of this *ziyārah* is as follows:

أَلسَّلَامُ عَلَيْكِ يَا بِنْتَ رَسُولِ اللّٰهِ.

Peace be upon you, O daughter of the Messenger of Allah.

أَلسَّلَامُ عَلَيْكِ يَا بِنْتَ نَبِيِّ اللّٰهِ.

Peace be upon you, O daughter of the Prophet of Allah.

أَلسَّلَامُ عَلَيْكِ يَا بِنْتَ حَبِيبِ اللّٰهِ.

Peace be upon you, O daughter of the most beloved one of Allah.

أَلسَّلَامُ عَلَيْكِ يَا بِنْتَ خَلِيلِ اللّٰهِ.

Peace be upon you, O daughter of the close friend of Allah.

أَلسَّلَامُ عَلَيْكِ يَا بِنْتَ صَفِيِّ اللّٰهِ.

Peace be upon you, O daughter of the chosen one of Allah.

أَلسَّلَامُ عَلَيْكِ يَا بِنْتَ أَمِينِ اللّٰهِ.

Peace be upon you, O daughter of the trustee of Allah.

أَلسَّلَامُ عَلَيْكِ يَا بِنْتَ خَيْرِ خَلْقِ اللّٰهِ.

Peace be upon you, O daughter of the best of Allah's creations.

أَلسَّلَامُ عَلَيْكِ يَا بِنْتَ أَفْضَلِ أَنْبِيَآءِ اللّٰهِ وَرُسُلِهِ وَمَلآئِكَتِهِ.

Peace be upon you, O daughter of the best of the Prophets of Allah, and His Messengers, and His Angels.

أَلسَّلَامُ عَلَيْكِ يَا بِنْتَ خَيْرِ الْبَرِيَّةِ.

Peace be upon you, O daughter of the best of created beings.

أَلسَّلَامُ عَلَيْكِ يَا سَيِّدَةَ نِسَآءِ الْعَالَمِينَ مِنَ الْأَوَّلِينَ وَالْآخِرِينَ.

Peace be upon you, O the Leader of all women of the world, including the past and the future generations.

أَلسَّلَامُ عَلَيْكِ يَا زَوْجَةَ وَلِيِّ اللّٰهِ وَخَيْرِ الْخَلْقِ بَعْدَ رَسُولِ اللّٰهِ.

Peace be upon you, O the wife of the guardian of (the message) of Allah and the best of all created beings after the Messenger of Allah.

أَلسَّلَامُ عَلَيْكِ يَا أُمَّ الْحَسَنِ وَالْحُسَيْنِ،

Peace be upon you, O the mother of Ḥasan and Ḥusayn,

سَيِّدَيْ شَبَابِ أَهْلِ الْجَنَّةِ.

The two masters of the youth of Paradise.

أَلسَّلَامُ عَلَيْكِ أَيَّتُهَا الصِّدِّيقَةُ الشَّهِيدَةُ.

Peace be upon you, O the Veracious *(al-Ṣiddīqa)*, the martyred *(al-Shahīda)*.

أَلسَّلَامُ عَلَيْكِ أَيَّتُهَا الرَّضِيَّةُ الْمَرْضِيَّةُ.

Peace be upon you, O the Content *(al-Raḍīyya)*, the pleased *(al-Marḍiyya)*.

أَلسَّلَامُ عَلَيْكِ أَيَّتُهَا الْفَاضِلَةُ الزَّكِيَّةُ.

Peace be upon you, O the Virtuous *(al-Fādhila)*, the Pure *(al-Zakiyya)*.

أَلسَّلَامُ عَلَيْكِ أَيَّتُهَا الْحَوْرَآءُ الإِنْسِيَّةُ.

Peace be upon you, O the Paradisiacal human being *(al-Ḥawrā' al-Insiyya)*.

أَلسَّلَامُ عَلَيْكِ أَيَّتُهَا التَّقِيَّةُ النَّقِيَّةُ.

Peace be upon you, O the Pious *(al-Taqiyya)*, the Immaculate *(al-Naqiyya)*.

أَلسَّلَامُ عَلَيْكِ أَيَّتُهَا الْمُحَدَّثَةُ الْعَلِيمَةُ.

Peace be upon you, O the one whom the angels spoke to *(al-Muḥaddatha)*, the Knowledgeable one *(al-'Alīma)*.

أَلسَّلَامُ عَلَيْكِ أَيَّتُهَا الْمَظْلُومَةُ الْمَغْصُوبَةُ.

Peace be upon you, O the Oppressed lady *(al-Maẓlūma)* whose right was usurped *(al-Maghṣūba)*.

أَلسَّلَامُ عَلَيْكِ أَيَّتُهَا الْمُضْطَهَدَةُ الْمَقْهُورَةُ.

Peace be upon you, O the Persecuted *(al-Muḍṭahada)*, the Maltreated *(al-Maqhūra)*.

أَلسَّلَامُ عَلَيْكِ يَا فَاطِمَةُ بِنْتَ رَسُولِ اللّٰهِ،

Peace be upon you, O Fāṭima, daughter of the Messenger of Allah,

وَرَحْمَةُ اللّٰهِ وَبَرَكَاتُهُ.

And the mercy and blessings of Allah (be upon you).

صَلَّى اللّٰهُ عَلَيْكِ،

May Allah send His prayers upon you,

وَعَلَىٰ رُوحِكِ وَبَدَنِكِ.

And your soul, and your body.

أَشْهَدُ أَنَّكِ مَضَيْتِ عَلَىٰ بَيِّنَةٍ مِنْ رَبِّكِ.

I bear witness that you spent your (entire) life with full awareness of your duty towards your Lord.

وَأَنَّ مَنْ سَرَّكِ فَقَدْ سَرَّ رَسُولَ اللّٰهِ صَلَّى اللّٰهُ عَلَيْهِ وَآلِهِ،

And (I bear witness) that one who pleases you, will have pleased the Messenger of Allah - blessings of Allāh be upon him and his family,

وَمَنْ جَفَاكِ فَقَدْ جَفَا رَسُولَ اللّٰهِ صَلَّى اللّٰهُ عَلَيْهِ وَآلِهِ،

And the one who displeases you will have displeased the Messenger of Allah - blessings of Allāh be upon him and his family,

وَمَنْ آذَاكِ فَقَدْ آذَى رَسُولَ اللّٰهِ صَلَّى اللّٰهُ عَلَيْهِ وَآلِهِ،

And the one who harms you will have harmed the Messenger of Allah - blessings of Allāh be upon him and his family,

وَمَنْ وَصَلَكِ فَقَدْ وَصَلَ رَسُولَ اللّٰهِ صَلَّى اللّٰهُ عَلَيْهِ وَآلِهِ،

And the one who respects you will have respected the Messenger of Allah - peace be upon him and his family,

وَمَنْ قَطَعَكِ فَقَدْ قَطَعَ رَسُولَ اللّٰهِ صَلَّى اللّٰهُ عَلَيْهِ وَآلِهِ،

And the one who disrespects you will have disrespected the Messenger of Allah - blessings of Allāh be upon him and his family,

لِأَنَّكِ بِضْعَةٌ مِنْهُ،

This is because you are an inseparable part of him (the Prophet),

وَرُوحُهُ الَّذِي بَيْنَ جَنْبَيْهِ.

And you are his soul with which he lives.

أُشْهِدُ اللّٰهَ وَمَلآئِكَتَهُ أَنِّي وَلِيٌّ لِمَنْ وَالاَكِ،

I ask Allah and His angels to be the witnesses that I am the friend of one who adheres to you,

وَعَدُوٌّ لِمَنْ عَادَاكِ،

And I am the enemy to one who is an enemy of you,

وَحَرْبٌ لِمَنْ حَارَبَكِ.

And I am at war against one who wages war against you.

أَنَا يَا مَوْلاَتِي بِكِ وَبِأَبِيكِ وَبَعْلِكِ وَالأَئِمَّةِ مِنْ وُلْدِكِ مُوقِنٌ،

O my master! I have full faith in you, your father, your husband, and your sons - the Imāms,

وَبِوِلاَيَتِهِمْ مُؤْمِنٌ،

And I believe in their (Divinely-commissioned) leadership,

وَلِطَاعَتِهِمْ مُلْتَزِمٌ.

And I commit myself to their obedience.

أَشْهَدُ أَنَّ الدِّينَ دِينُهُمْ،

I bear witness that their religion is the true religion,

وَالْحُكْمَ حُكْمُهُمْ،

And their command is the true command,

وَهُمْ قَدْ بَلَّغُوا عَنِ اللهِ عَزَّ وَجَلَّ،

And they have conveyed (the message) on behalf of Allah, and Grand and Majestic,

وَدَعَوْا إِلىٰ سَبِيلِ اللّٰهِ بِالْحِكْمَةِ وَالْـمَوْعِظَةِ الْـحَسَنَةِ.

And they have called to the Way of Allah with wisdom and fair exhortation.

لاَ تَأْخُذُهُمْ فِي اللّٰهِ لَوْمَةُ لاَئِمٍ.

They have never feared the blame of anyone concerning carrying out their duties towards Allah.

وَصَلَوَاتُ اللّٰهِ عَلَيْكِ وَعَلىٰ أَبِيكِ وَبَعْلِكِ،

Blessings of Allah be upon you, and upon your father, and your husband,

وَذُرِّيَّتِكِ الأَئِمَّةِ الطَّاهِرِينَ.

And your descendants - the Immaculate Imāms.

أَللّٰهُمّ صَلِّ عَلىٰ مُحَمَّدٍ وَأَهْلِ بَيْتِهِ،

O Allah, send blessings upon Muḥammad and his Household,

وَصَلِّ عَلىٰ الْبَتُولِ الطَّاهِرَةِ،

And upon the Immaculate *(al-Batūl)*, the Pure lady *(al-Ṭāhira)*,

أَلصِّدِّيقَةِ الْـمَعْصُومَةِ،

The Veracious *(al-Ṣiddīqa)*, the Sinless *(al-Maʿṣūma)*,

أَلتَّقِيَّةِ النَّقِيَّةِ،

The Pious *(al-Taqiyya)*, the Immaculate *(al-Naqiyya)*,

أَلرَّضِيَّةِ الْـمَرْضِيَّةِ،

The Content *(al-Raḍīyya)*, the Well-pleased *(al-Marḍīyya)*,

الزَّكِيَّةِ الرَّشِيدَةِ،

The Chaste *(al-Zakiyya)*, the Rightly-guided *(al-Rashīda)*,

الْمَظْلُومَةِ الْمَقْهُورَةِ،

The Oppressed *(al-Maẓlūma)*, the Wronged *(al-Maqhūra)*,

الْمَغْصُوبَةِ حَقُّهَا،

The one whose rights were usurped,

الْمَمْنُوعَةِ إِرْثُهَا،

The one whose right of inheritance was violated,

الْمَكْسُورَةِ ضِلْعُهَا،

The one whose rib was broken,

الْمَظْلُومِ بَعْلُهَا،

The one whose husband was oppressed,

الْمَقْتُولِ وَلَدُهَا،

The one whose son was slain.

فَاطِمَةَ بِنْتِ رَسُولِكَ،

(She is) Fāṭima: the daughter of Your Messenger,

وَبَضْعَةِ لَحْمِهِ،

And part of his flesh,

وَصَمِيمِ قَلْبِهِ،

And essence of his heart,

وَفِلْذَةِ كَبِدِهِ،

And piece of his innermost,

وَالنَّخْبَةِ مِنْكَ لَهُ،

And choice of You for him,

وَالتُّحْفَةِ خَصَصْتَ بِهَا وَصِيَّهُ،

And gift that You gave exclusively to his (the Prophet's) successor,

وَحَبِيبَةِ الْـمُصْطَفىٰ،

And most beloved of the Chosen Prophet *(al-Muṣṭafā)*,

وَقَرِينَةِ الْـمُرْتَضىٰ،

And wife of the Chosen One *(al-Murtaḍā)*,

وَسَيِّدَةِ النِّسَآءِ،

And Leader of all the women,

وَمُبَشِّرَةِ الأَوْلِيَآءِ،

And conveyor of good tidings to the intimate servants (of Allah),

حَلِيفَةِ الْوَرَعِ وَالزُّهْدِ،

Ahe inseparable one from piety and asceticism,

وَتُفَّاحَةِ الْفِرْدَوْسِ وَالْـخُلْدِ،

And the apple of Heaven (*Firdaus*) and eternity (in Paradise),

أَلَّتِي شَرَّفْتَ مَوْلِدَهَا بِنِسَآءِ الْـجَنَّةِ،

(The lady) through whose birth You have honoured the women of Paradise,

وَسَلَلْتَ مِنْهَا أَنْوَارَ الأَئِمَّةِ،

And from whom You pulled the Lights of the Imāms,

وَأَرْخَيْتَ دُونَـهَا حِجَابَ النُّبُوَّةِ.

And fixed the veil of Prophethood.

أَللّٰهُمَّ صَلِّ عَلَيْهَا صَلاَةً تَزِيدُ فِي مَـحَلِّهَا عِنْدَكَ،

O Allah, blessings be upon her, the blessings that raise her standing with You,

وَشَرَفِهَا لَدَيْكَ،

And her honour with You,

وَمَنْزِلَتِهَا مِنْ رِضَاكَ،

And raise her position in Your Pleasure,

وَبَلِّغْهَا مِنَّا تَـحِيَّةً وَسَلاَمًا،

And convey to her from us greetings and salutations,

وَآتِنَا مِنْ لَدُنْكَ فِي حُبِّهَا فَضْلاً وَإِحْسَانًا وَرَحْـمَةً وَغُفْرَانًا،

And grant us favour, kindness, mercy, and forgiveness from You on account of our love for her.

إِنَّكَ ذُو الْعَفْوِ الْكَرِيمِ.

Verily, You are the All-Generous Lord of forgiveness.

Ziyārah for the 3rd of Jumādī al-Ākhir

أَلسَّلَامُ عَلَيْكِ يَا سَيِّدَةَ نِسَآءِ الْعَالَـمِينَ.

Peace be upon you, O Leader of the women of the world.

أَلسَّلَامُ عَلَيْكِ يَا وَالِدَةَ الْـحُجَجِ عَلَىٰ النَّاسِ أَجْـمَعِينَ.

Peace be upon you, O the mother of the Proofs over all people.

أَلسَّلَامُ عَلَيْكِ أَيَّتُهَا الْـمَظْلُومَةُ الْـمَمْنُوعَةُ حَقُّهَا.

Peace be upon you, O the wronged one whose right was usurped.

أَللّٰهُمَّ صَلِّ عَلَىٰ أَمَتِكَ وَابْنَةِ نَبِيِّكَ وَزَوجَةِ وَصِيِّ نَبِيِّكَ،

O Allah, send blessings upon Your servant, the daughter of Your Prophet, and the wife of the successor of Your Prophet,

صَلَاةً تُزْلِفُهَا فَوْقَ زُلْفىٰ عِبَادِكَ الْـمُكَرَّمِينَ،

Such remarkable blessings that approach her nearer to You than the steps (of proximity taken by) Your honoured servants,

مِنْ أَهْلِ السَّمَاوَاتِ وَأَهْلِ الأَرْضِينَ.

From among the inhabitants of the Heavens and the Earth.

Ziyārah on Sunday

أَلسَّلَامُ عَلَيْكِ يَا مُـمْتَحَنَةُ.

Peace be on you, O the carefully examined one.

إِمْتَحَنَكِ الَّذِي خَلَقَكِ فَوَجَدَكِ لِـمَا امْتَحَنَكِ صَابِرَةً.

Allah examined (tried) you before He created you (for this worldly life), thus He found you successfully enduring in that trial.

أَنَا لَكِ مُصَدِّقٌ صَابِرٌ عَلىٰ مَا أَتَى بِهِ أَبُوكِ وَوَصِيُّهُ،

I believe in you; and I patiently bear all that which has been conveyed by your father and his successor,

صَلَوَاتُ اللهِ عَلَيْهِمْ.

Blessings of Allah be upon them.

وَأَنَا أَسْأَلُكِ إِنْ كُنْتُ صَدَّقْتُكِ إِلاَّ أَلْـحَقْتِنِي بِتَصْدِيقِي لَـهُمْ،

And I beseech you, if I have stated the truth, to bind me together with the testimony concerning them,

لِتُسَرِّ نَفْسِي.

To give joy (and satisfaction) to my soul.

فَاشْهَدِي أَنِّي طَاهِرٌ بِوَلَايَتِكِ وَوِلَايَةِ آلِ بَيْتِكِ،

So, bear witness that truly I am pure in your *walāya* and the *walāya* of your immaculate household,

صَلَوَاتُ اللهِ عَلَيْهِمْ أَجْـمَعِينَ.

Blessings of Allah be upon all of them.

Other Publications Available[102]

1. *A Land Most Goodly: The Story of Yemen in the Quran and in the Times of Prophet Muḥammad and Imam ʿAlī ibn Abī Ṭālib,* by Jaffer Ladak
2. *A Star Amongst the Stars: The life and times of the great companion: Jabir ibn Abdullah al-Ansari,* by Jaffer Ladak
3. *Alif, Baa, Taa of Kerbala,* by Saleem Bhimji, and Arifa Hudda
4. *Arbāʿīn of Imam Ḥusayn,* compiled and translated by Saleem Bhimji
5. *Daily Devotions,* compiled and translated by Saleem Bhimji
6. *Deficient? A Review of Sermon 80 from Nahj al-Balāgha,* by Āyatullāh al-ʿUẓmā Shaykh Nāṣir Makārim Shīrāzī and translated by Saleem Bhimji
7. *Exegesis of the 29th Juz of the Quran - a translation of Tafsīr Namuneh,* by Āyatullāh al-ʿUẓmā Shaykh Nāṣir Makārim Shīrāzī and translated by Saleem Bhimji
8. *Foundations of Islamic Unity* - a translation of *Al-Fuṣūl al-Muhimmah fī Ta'līf al-Ummah,* by ʿAbd al-Ḥusayn Sharaf al-Dīn al-Mūsawī al-ʿĀmilī and translated by Batool Ispahany
9. *Fountain of Paradise - Fāṭima az-Zahrā' in the Noble Quran,* by Āyatullāh al-ʿUẓmā Shaykh Nāṣir Makārim Shīrāzī, compiled and translated by Saleem Bhimji
10. *God and god of Science,* by Syed Hasan Raza Jafri

---

[102] The following is a list of all original writings and translations available from the **Islamic Publishing House**. As most of these titles are now out of stock, we are re-releasing all our works through **Amazon**. Search for the title that you are looking for via Amazon on any of their international platforms, including: Australia, Canada, France, Germany, Italy, Japan, UK, USA, Netherlands, and Spain.

11. *House of Sorrows,* by Shaykh ʿAbbās al-Qummī and translated by Aejaz Ali Turab Husayn Husayni
12. *Inspirational Insights,* by Mohammed Khaku
13. *Islam and Religious Pluralism,* by Āyatullāh Shaykh Murtaḍā Muṭahharī and translated by Sayyid Sulayman Ali Hasan
14. *Journey to Eternity - A Handbook of Supplications for the Soul,* compiled and translated by Saleem Bhimji and Arifa Hudda
15. *Love and Hate for Allah's Sake,* by Mujtaba Saburi translated by Saleem Bhimji
16. *Love for the Family,* compiled and translated by Yasin T. Al-Jibouri, Saleem Bhimji, and others
17. *Moral Management,* by Abbas Rahimi and translated by Saleem Bhimji
18. *Morals of the Masumeen,* by Arifa Hudda
19. *Prayers of the Final Prophet - A Collection of Supplications of Prophet Muḥammad,* by ʿAllāmah Sayyid Muḥammad Ḥusayn Ṭabāʾṭabāʾī and translated by Tahir Ridha-Jaffer
20. *Prospering Through a Cost of Living Crisis,* by Jaffer Ladak
21. *Ramaḍān Reflections,* compiled by A Group of Muslim Scholars and translated by Saleem Bhimji
22. *Ṣalāt al-Āyāt,* by Saleem Bhimji
23. *Ṣalāt al-Ghufaylah: Salvation through Patience & Perseverance,* written by Saleem Bhimji
24. *Secrets of the Ḥajj,* by Āyatullāh al-ʿUẓmā Shaykh Ḥusayn Mazāherī and translated by Saleem Bhimji
25. *Sunan an-Nabī,* by ʿAllāmah Sayyid Muḥammad Ḥusayn Ṭabāʾṭabāʾī and translated by Tahir Ridha-Jaffer
26. *Tears from Heaven's Flowers: An Anthology of English Poetry about the Ahlulbayt,* by Abrahim al-Zubeidi

27. *The Firmest Armament: Commentary on Āyatul Kursī (The Verse of the Throne),* by Sayyid Nasrullah Burujerdi and translated by Saleem Bhimji
28. *The Last Luminary and Ways to Delve into the Light,* by Sayyid Muhammad Ridha Husayni Mutlaq and translated by Saleem Bhimji
29. *The Muslim Legal Will Booklet,* by Saleem Bhimji
30. *The Pure Life,* by Āyatullāh al-ʿUẓmā as-Sayyid Muḥammad Taqī al-Modarresī and translated by Jaffer Ladak with commentary by Dr. Zainali Panjwani and Jaffer Ladak
31. *The Tragedy of Kerbalāʾ,* as narrated by Imam ʿAlī ibn al-Ḥusayn al-Sajjād, recorded by Shaykh al-Ṣadūq and translated by ʿAbdul Zahrāʾ ʿAbdul Ḥusayn
32. *The Third Testimony: Imam ʿAlī in the Adhān,* compiled and translated by Saleem Bhimji
33. *The Torch of Perpetual Guidance - A Brief Commentary on Ziyārat al-ʿĀshūrāʾ,* by Abbas Azizi and translated by Saleem Bhimji
34. *Weapon of the Believer,* by ʿAllāmah Muḥammad Bāqir Majlisī and translated by Saleem Bhimji

In addition to the above, our *Living The Quran Through The Living Quran* series of commentary on the Noble Quran is also being published. To date, we have released the commentary of:

1. Sūrah al-Najm (53)
2. Sūrah Qāf (50)

The commentary of the following chapters of the Quran will also be released in the future:

1. Sūrah al-Fātiḥa (1)
2. Sūrah Yāsīn (36)
3. Sūrah al-Wāqiʿah (56)
4. Sūrah al-Mujādilah (58)
5. Sūrah al-Ṣaff (61)

This series of booklets will be available exclusively from Amazon.

www.ingramcontent.com/pod-product-compliance
Lightning Source LLC
Chambersburg PA
CBHW032134040426
42449CB00005B/240
* 9 7 8 1 9 2 7 9 3 0 5 1 9 *